本书出版得到《大中华文库》出版经费资助

大中华文库
LIBRARY
OF CHINESE CLASSICS

学术顾问委员会：(按姓氏笔画排序)

丁往道　叶水夫　任继愈　刘重德
汤博文　李学勤　李赋宁　杨宪益
沙博理　季羡林　林戊荪　金开诚
胡文仲　徐公持　袁行霈　梁良兴
韩素音　戴文葆

总监纂委员会

总　监　纂：龙新民
副总监纂：(按姓氏笔画排序)
于友先　邬书林　刘　杲　杨牧之
陈满之　金立群　蔡名照

工作委员会：

主　　任：杨牧之
副　主　任：黄友义　阎晓宏
　　　　　张少春　张光华
　　　　　吴尚之
委　　员：(按姓氏笔画排序)
王显臣　王国臣　刘国玉　刘玉山
李　岩　李建国　李朋义　李　峰
李鹏青　陈万雄　杨德炎　肖晓明
张增顺　张海鸥　周洪力　周奎杰
胡国臣　顾爱彬　秦　颖　萧启明
黄　松　曾主陶　熊治祁

编辑委员会：

总　编　辑：杨牧之
副总编辑：(按姓氏笔画排序)
马欣来　尹飞舟　王家新
肖晓明　徐明强　黄友义

装帧设计：廖　铁
印装监制：李　坦　李　林　韩少乙

Academic Consulting Committee:
Ding Wangdao, Ye Shuifu,
Ren Jiyu, Liu Zhongde, Tang Bowen,
Li Xueqin, Li Funing, Yang Xianyi,
Sidney Shapiro, Ji Xianlin, Lin Wusun,
Jin Kaicheng, Hu Wenzhong,
Xu Gongchi, Yuan Xingpei,
Liang Liangxing, Han Suyin, Dai Wenbao

Compilation Supervising Committee:
Compilation Supervisor: Long Xinmin
Compilation Co-Supervisors: Yu Youxian,
Wu Shulin, Liu Gao, Yang Muzhi,
Chen Manzhi, Jin Liqun, Cai Mingzhao

Working Committee:
Chairman: Yang Muzhi
Vice-Chairmen:
Huang Youyi, Yan Xiaohong,
Zhang Shaochun, Zhang Guanghua,
Wu Shangzhi
Members:
Wang Xianchen, Wang Guochen,
Liu Guoyu, Liu Yushan, Li Yan,
Li Jianguo, Li Pengyi, Li Feng,
Li Pengqing, Chen Wanxiong,
Yang Deyan, Xiao Xiaoming,
Zhang Zengshun, Zhang Hai'ou,
Zhou Hongli, Zhou Kuijie, Hu Guochen,
Gu Aibin, Qin Ying, Xiao Qiming,
Huang Song, Zeng Zhutao,
Xiong Zhiqi

Editorial Committee:
Chief-Editor: Yang Muzhi
Deputy Chief-Editors:
Ma Xinlai, Yin Feizhou,
Wang Jiaxin, Xiao Xiaoming,
Xu Mingqiang, Huang Youyi

Designers: Liao Tie
Production Controllers:
Li Tan, Li Lin, Han Shaoyi

大中华文库

汉英对照

LIBRARY OF CHINESE CLASSICS

Chinese-English

新编千家诗

GEMS OF CLASSICAL CHINESE POETRY

袁行霈　编

许渊冲　英译　　徐放　韩珊　今译

Compiler by Yuan XingPei

Translated into English by Xu Yuan Zhong

Translated into Modern Chinese by Xu Fang　Han Shan

中　华　书　局

Zhonghua Book Company

Beijing, China

First Edition 2006

All rights reserved. No part of this publication may be reproduced or transmitted in any form or by any means, electronic or mechanical, now known or to be invented, without permission in writing from the publishers, except for brief quotations by reviewers.

ISBN 7-101-04940-0/I·672
©2006 Zhonghua Book Company

Published by
Zhonghua Book Company
  38 TaiPing Qiao Xi Li,
  Feng Tai District,
  Beijing, China
  http://www.zhbc.com.cn
Printed by
Shenzhen Jiaxinda Printing Co.,Ltd.,Shenzhen,China
Printed in the People's Republic of China

总　序

杨牧之

《大中华文库》终于出版了。我们为之高兴，为之鼓舞，但也倍感压力。

当此之际，我们愿将郁积在我们心底的话，向读者倾诉。

一

中华民族有着悠久的历史和灿烂的文化，系统、准确地将中华民族的文化经典翻译成外文，编辑出版，介绍给全世界，是几代中国人的愿望。早在几十年前，西方一位学者翻译《红楼梦》，书名译成《一个红楼上的梦》，将林黛玉译为"黑色的玉"。我们一方面对外国学者将中国的名著介绍到世界上去表示由衷的感谢，一方面为祖国的名著还不被完全认识，甚而受到曲解，而感到深深的遗憾。还有西方学者翻译《金瓶梅》，专门摘选其中自然主义描述最为突出的篇章加以译介。一时间，西方学者好像发现了奇迹，掀起了《金瓶梅》热，说中国是"性开放的源头"，公开地在报刊上鼓吹中国要"发扬开放之传统"。还有许多资深、友善的汉学家译介中国古代的哲学著作，在把中华民族文化介绍给全世界的工作方面作出了重大贡献，但或囿于理解有误，或缘于对中国文字认识的局限，质量上乘的并不多，常常是隔靴搔痒，说不到点子上。大哲学家黑格尔曾经说过：中国有最完备的国史。但他认为中国古代没有真正意义上的哲学，还处在哲学史前状态。这么了不起的哲学家竟然作出这样大失水准的评论，何其不幸。正如任何哲学家都要受时间、地点、条件的制约一样，黑格尔也离不开这一规律。当时他也只能从上述水平的汉学家译过去的文字去分析、理解，所以，黑格尔先生对中国古代社会的认识水平是什么状态，也就不难想象了。

中国离不开世界，世界也缺少不了中国。中国文化摄取外域的新成分，丰富了自己，又以自己的新成就输送给别人，贡献于世界。从公元5世纪开始到公元15世纪，大约有一千年，中国走在世界的前列。在这一千多年的时间里，她的光辉照耀全世界。人类要前进，怎么能不全面认识中国，怎么能不认真研究中国的历史呢？

二

中华民族是伟大的，曾经辉煌过，蓝天、白云、阳光灿烂，和平而兴旺；也有过黑暗的、想起来就让人战栗的日子，但中华民族从来是充满理想，不断追求，不断学习，渴望和平与友谊的。

中国古代伟大的思想家孔子曾经说过："三人行，必有我师焉。择其善者而从之，其不善者而改之。"孔子的话就是要人们向别人学习。这段话正是概括了整个中华民族与人交往的原则。人与人之间交往如此，在与周边的国家交往中也是如此。

秦始皇第一个统一了中国，可惜在位只有十几年，来不及作更多的事情。汉朝继秦而继续强大，便开始走出去，了解自己周边的世界。公元前138年，汉武帝派张骞出使西域。他带着一万头牛羊，总值一万万钱的金帛货物，作为礼物，开始西行，最远到过"安息"(即波斯)。公元前36年，班超又率36人出使西域。36个人按今天的话说，也只有一个排，显然是为了拜访未曾见过面的邻居，是去交朋友。到了西域，班超派遣甘英作为使者继续西行，往更远处的大秦国(即罗马)去访问，"乃抵条支而历安息，临西海以望大秦"(《后汉书·西域传》)。"条支"在"安息"以西，即今天的伊拉克、叙利亚一带，"西海"应是今天的地中海。也就是说甘英已经到达地中海边上，与罗马帝国隔海相望，"临大海欲渡"，却被人劝阻而未成行，这在历史上留下了遗恨。可以想见班超、甘英沟通友谊的无比勇气和强烈愿望。接下来是唐代的玄奘，历经千难万险，到"西天"印度取经，带回了南亚国家的古老文化。归国后，他把带回的佛教经典组织人翻译，到后来很多经典印度失传了，但中国却保存完好，以至于今天，没有玄奘的《大唐西域记》，印度人很难编写印度古代史。明代郑和"七下西洋"，把中华文化传到东南亚一带。鸦片战争以后，一代又一代先进的中国人，为了振兴中华，又前赴后继，向西方国家学习先进的科学思想和文明成果。这中间有我们的领导人朱德、周恩来、邓小平；有许许多多大科学家、文学家、艺术家，如郭沫若、李四光、钱学森、冼星海、徐悲鸿等。他们的追求、奋斗，他们的博大胸怀，兼收并蓄的精神，为人类社会增添了光彩。

中国文化的形成和发展过程，就是一个以众为师，以各国人民为师，不断学习和创造的过程。中华民族曾经向周边国家和民族学习过许多东西，假如没有这些学习，中华民族决不可能创造出昔日的辉煌。回顾历史，我们怎么能够不对伟大的古埃及文明、古希腊文明、古印度文明满怀深深的感激？怎么能够不对伟大的欧洲文明、非洲文明、美洲文明、澳洲文明，以及中国周围的亚洲文明充满温情与敬意？

中华民族为人类社会曾作出过独特的贡献。在15世纪以前，中国的科学技术一直处于世界遥遥领先的地位。英国科学家李约瑟说："中国在公元3世纪到13世纪之间，保持着一个西方所望尘莫及的科学知识水平。"美国耶鲁大学教授、《大国的兴衰》的作者保罗·肯尼迪坦言："在近代以前时期的所有文明中，没有一个国家的文明比中国更发达，更先进。"

世界各国的有识之士千里迢迢来中国观光、学习。在这个过程中，中国唐朝的长安城渐渐发展成为国际大都市。西方的波斯、东罗马，东亚的高丽、新罗、百济、南天竺、北天竺，频繁前来。外国的王侯、留学生，在长安供职的外国官员，商贾、乐工和舞士，总有几十个国家，几万人之多。日本派出"遣唐使"更是一批接一批。传为美谈的日本人阿部仲麻吕（晁衡）在长安留学的故事，很能说明外国人与中国的交往。晁衡学成仕于唐朝，前后历时五十余年。晁衡与中国的知识分子结下了深厚的友情。他归国时，传说在海中遇难身亡。大诗人李白作诗哭悼："日本晁卿辞帝都，征帆一片远蓬壶。明月不归沉碧海，白云愁色满苍梧。"晁衡遇险是误传，但由此可见中外学者之间在中国长安交往的情谊。

后来，不断有外国人到中国来探寻秘密，所见所闻，常常让他们目瞪口呆。《希腊纪事》（希腊人波桑尼阿著）记载公元2世纪时，希腊人在中国的见闻。书中写道："赛里斯人用小米和青芦喂一种类似蜘蛛的昆虫，喂到第五年，虫肚子胀裂开，便从里面取出丝来。"从这段对中国古代养蚕技术的描述，可见当时欧洲人与中国人的差距。公元9世纪中叶，阿拉伯人来到中国。一位阿拉伯作家在他所著的《中国印度闻见录》中记载了曾旅居中国的阿拉伯商人的见闻：

——一天，一个外商去拜见驻守广州的中国官吏。会见时，外商总盯着官吏的胸部，官吏很奇怪，便问："你好像总盯着我的胸，这是怎么回事？"那位外商回答说："透过你穿的丝绸衣服，我隐约看到你胸口上长着一个黑痣，这是什么丝绸，我感到十分惊奇。"官吏听后，失声大笑，伸出胳膊，说："请你数数吧，看我穿了几件衣服？"那商人数过，竟然穿了五件之多，黑痣正是透过这五层丝绸衣服显现出来的。外商惊得目瞪口呆，官吏说："我穿的丝绸还不算是最好的，总督穿的要更精美。"

——书中关于茶(他们叫干草叶子)的记载，可见阿拉伯国家当时还没有喝茶的习惯。书中记述："中国国王本人的收入主要靠盐税和泡开水喝的一种干草税。在各个城市里，这种干草叶售价都很高，中国人称这种草叶叫'茶'，这种干草叶比苜蓿的叶子还多，也略比它香，稍有苦味，用开水冲喝，治百病。"

——他们对中国的医疗条件十分羡慕，书中记载道："中国人医疗条件很好，穷人可以从国库中得到药费。"还说："城市里，很多地方立一石碑，高10肘，上面刻有各种疾病和药物，写明某种病用某种药医治。"

——关于当时中国的京城，书中作了生动的描述：中国的京城很大，人口众多，一条宽阔的长街把全城分为两半，大街右边的东区，住着皇帝、宰相、禁军及皇家的总管、奴婢。在这个区域，沿街开凿了小河，流水潺潺；路旁，葱茏的树木整然有序，一幢幢宅邸鳞次栉比。大街左边的西区，住着庶民和商人。这里有货栈和商店,每当清晨,人们可以看到,皇室的总管、宫廷的仆役,或骑马或步行,到这里来采购。

此后的史籍对西人来华的记载,渐渐多了起来。13世纪意大利旅行家马可·波罗,尽管有人对他是否真的到过中国持怀疑态度,但他留下一部记述元代事件的《马可·波罗游记》却是确凿无疑的。这部游记中的一些关于当时中国的描述使得西方人认为是"天方夜谭"。总之,从中西文化交流史来说,这以前的时期还是一个想象和臆测的时代,相互之间充满了好奇与幻想。

从16世纪末开始,由于航海技术的发展,东西方航路的开通,随着一批批传教士来华,中国与西方开始了直接的交流。沟通中西的使命在意大利传教士利玛窦那里有了充分的体现。利玛窦于1582年来华,1610年病逝于北京,在华20余年。除了传教以外,做了两件具有历史象征意义的事,一是1594年前后在韶州用拉丁文翻译《四书》,并作了注释;二是与明代学者徐光启合作,用中文翻译了《几何原本》。

西方传教士对《四书》等中国经典的粗略翻译,以及杜赫德的《中华帝国志》等书对中国的介绍,在西方读者的眼前展现了一个异域文明,在当时及稍后一段时期引起了一场"中国热",许多西方大思想家的眼光都曾注目中国文化。有的推崇中华文明,如莱布尼兹、伏尔泰、魁奈等,有的对中华文明持批评态度,如孟德斯鸠、黑格尔等。莱布尼兹认识到中国文化的某些思想与他的观念相近,如周易的卦象与他发明的二进制相契合,对中国文化给予了热情的礼赞;黑格尔则从他整个哲学体系的推演出发,认为中国没有真正意义上的哲学,还处在哲学史前的状态。但是,不论是推崇还是批评，是吸纳还是排斥，中西文化的交流产生了巨大的影响。随着先进的中国科学技术的西传，特别是中国的造纸、火药、印刷术和指南针四大发明的问世，大大改变了世界的面貌。马克思说："中国的火药把骑士阶层炸得粉碎，指南针打开了世界市场并建立了殖民地，而印刷术则变成了新教的工具，变成对精神发展创造必要前提的最强大的杠杆。"英国的哲学家培根说：中国的四大发明"改变了全世界的面貌和一切事物的状态"。

三

大千世界，潮起潮落。云散云聚，万象更新。中国古代产生了无数伟大科学家：祖冲之、李时珍、孙思邈、张衡、沈括、毕升……，产生了无数科技成果:《齐民要术》、《九章算术》、《伤寒杂病论》、《本草纲目》……，以及保存至今的世界奇迹：浑天仪、地动仪、都江堰、敦煌石窟、大运河、万里长城……。但从15世纪下半叶起，风水似乎从东方转到了西方，落后的欧洲只经过400年便成为世界瞩目的文明中心。英国的牛顿、波兰的哥白尼、德国的伦琴、法国的居里、德国的爱因斯坦、意大利的伽利略、俄国的门捷列夫、美国的费米和爱迪生……，光芒四射，令人敬仰。

中华民族开始思考了。潮起潮落究竟是什么原因？中国人发明的火药，传到欧洲，转眼之间反成为欧洲列强轰击中国大门的炮弹，又是因为什么？

鸦片战争终于催醒了中国人沉睡的迷梦，最先"睁眼看世界"的一代精英林则徐、魏源迈出了威武雄壮的一步。曾国藩、李鸿章搞起了洋务运动。中国的知识分子喊出"民主与科学"的口号。中国是落后了,中国的志士仁人在苦苦探索。但落后中饱含着变革的动力,探索中孕育着崛起的希望。"向科学进军",中华民族终于又迎来了科学的春天。

今天,世界毕竟来到了21世纪的门槛。分散隔绝的世界,逐渐变成联系为一体的世界。现在,全球一体化趋势日益明显,人类历史也就在愈来愈大的程度上成为全世界的历史。当今,任何一种文化的发展都离不开对其它优秀文化的汲取,都以其它优秀文化的发展为前提。在近现代,西方文化汲取中国文化,不仅是中国文化的传播,更是西方文化自身的创新和发展;正如中国文化对西方文化的汲取一样,既是西方文化在中国的传播,同时也是中国文化在近代的转型和发展。地球上所有的人类文化,都是我们共同的宝贵遗产。既然我们生活的各个大陆,在地球史上曾经是连成一气的"泛大陆",或者说是一个完整的"地球村",那么,我们同样可以在这个以知识和学习为特征的网络时代,走上相互学习、共同发展的大路,建设和开拓我们人类崭新的"地球村"。

西学仍在东渐,中学也将西传。各国人民的优秀文化正日益迅速地为中国文化所汲取,而无论西方和东方,也都需要从中国文化中汲取养分。正是基于这一认识,我们组织出版汉英对照版《大中华文库》,全面系统地翻译介绍中国传统文化典籍。我们试图通过《大中华文库》,向全世界展示,中华民族五千年的追求,五千年的梦想,正在新的历史时期重放光芒。中国人民就像火后的凤凰,万众一心,迎接新世纪文明的太阳。

1999 年 8 月

PREFACE TO THE
LIBRARY OF CHINESE CLASSICS

Yang Muzhi

The publication of the *Library of Chinese Classics* is a matter of great satisfaction to all of us who have been involved in the production of this monumental work. At the same time, we feel a weighty sense of responsibility, and take this opportunity to explain to our readers the motivation for undertaking this cross-century task.

1

The Chinese nation has a long history and a glorious culture, and it has been the aspiration of several generations of Chinese scholars to translate, edit and publish the whole corpus of the Chinese literary classics so that the nation's greatest cultural achievements can be introduced to people all over the world. There have been many translations of the Chinese classics done by foreign scholars. A few dozen years ago, a Western scholar translated the title of *A Dream of Red Mansions* into "A Dream of Red Chambers" and Lin Daiyu, the heroine in the novel, into "Black Jade." But while their endeavours have been laudable, the results of their labours have been less than satisfactory. Lack of knowledge of Chinese culture and an inadequate grasp of the Chinese written language have led the translators into many errors. As a consequence, not only are Chinese classical writings widely misunderstood in the rest of the world, in some cases their content has actually been distorted. At one time, there was a "*Jin Ping Mei* craze" among Western scholars, who thought that they had uncovered a miraculous phenomenon, and published theories claiming that China was the "fountainhead of eroticism," and that a Chinese "tradition of permissiveness" was about to be laid bare. This distorted view came about due to the translators of the *Jin Ping Mei (Plum in the Golden Vase)* putting one-sided stress on the raw elements in that novel, to the neglect of its overall literary value. Meanwhile, there have been many distinguished and well-intentioned Sinologists who have attempted to make the culture of the Chinese nation more widely known by translating works of ancient Chinese philosophy. However, the quality of such work, in many cases, is unsatisfactory, often missing the point entirely. The great philosopher Hegel considered that ancient China had no philosophy in the real sense of the word, being stuck in philosophical "prehistory." For such an eminent authority to make such a colossal error of judgment is truly regrettable. But, of course, Hegel was just as subject to the constraints of time, space and other objective conditions as anyone else, and since he had to rely for his knowledge of Chinese philosophy on inadequate translations it is not difficult to imagine why he went so far off the mark.

China cannot be separated from the rest of the world; and the rest of the world cannot ignore China. Throughout its history, Chinese civilization has enriched itself by absorbing new elements from the outside world, and in turn has contributed to the progress of world civilization as a whole by transmitting to other peoples its own cultural achievements. From the 5th to the 15th centuries, China marched in the front ranks of world civilization. If mankind wishes to advance, how can it afford to ignore China? How can it afford not to make a thoroughgoing study of its history?

2

Despite the ups and downs in their fortunes, the Chinese people have always been idealistic, and have never ceased to forge ahead and learn from others, eager to strengthen ties of peace and friendship.

The great ancient Chinese philosopher Confucius once said, "Wherever three persons come together, one of them will surely be able to teach me something. I will pick out his good points and emulate them; his bad points I will reform." Confucius meant by this that we should always be ready to learn from others. This maxim encapsulates the principle the Chinese people have always followed in their dealings with other peoples, not only on an individual basis but also at the level of state-to-state relations.

After generations of internecine strife, China was unified by Emperor

Qin Shi Huang (the First Emperor of the Qin Dynasty) in 221 B.C. The Han Dynasty, which succeeded that of the short-lived Qin, waxed powerful, and for the first time brought China into contact with the outside world. In 138 B.C., Emperor Wu dispatched Zhang Qian to the western regions, i.e. Central Asia. Zhang, who traveled as far as what is now Iran, took with him as presents for the rulers he visited on the way 10,000 head of sheep and cattle, as well as gold and silks worth a fabulous amount. In 36 B.C., Ban Chao headed a 36-man legation to the western regions. These were missions of friendship to visit neighbours the Chinese people had never met before and to learn from them. Ban Chao sent Gan Ying to explore further toward the west. According to the "Western Regions Section" in the *Book of Later Han*, Gan Ying traveled across the territories of present-day Iraq and Syria, and reached the Mediterranean Sea, an expedition which brought him within the confines of the Roman Empire. Later, during the Tang Dynasty, the monk Xuan Zang made a journey fraught with danger to reach India and seek the knowledge of that land. Upon his return, he organized a team of scholars to translate the Buddhist scriptures, which he had brought back with him. As a result, many of these scriptural classics which were later lost in India have been preserved in China. In fact, it would have been difficult for the people of India to reconstruct their own ancient history if it had not been for Xuan Zang's *A Record of a Journey to the West in the Time of the Great Tang Dynasty*. In the Ming Dynasty, Zheng He transmitted Chinese culture to Southeast Asia during his seven voyages. Following the Opium Wars in the mid-19th century, progressive Chinese, generation after generation, went to study the advanced scientific thought and cultural achievements of the Western countries. Their aim was to revive the fortunes of their own country. Among them were people who were later to become leaders of China, including Zhu De, Zhou Enlai and Deng Xiaoping. In addition, there were people who were to become leading scientists, literary figures and artists, such as Guo Moruo, Li Siguang, Qian Xuesen, Xian Xinghai and Xu Beihong. Their spirit of ambition, their struggles and their breadth of vision were an inspiration not only to the Chinese people but to people all over the world.

Indeed, it is true that if the Chinese people had not learned many things from the surrounding countries they would never have been able to produce the splendid achievements of former days. When we look back upon history, how can we not feel profoundly grateful for the legacies of the civilizations of ancient Egypt, Greece and India? How can we not feel fondness and respect for the cultures of Europe, Africa, America and Oceania?

The Chinese nation, in turn, has made unique contributions to the community of mankind. Prior to the 15th century, China led the world in science and technology. The British scientist Joseph Needham once said, "From the third century A.D. to the 13th century A.D. China was far ahead of the West in the level of its scientific knowledge." Paul Kennedy, of Yale University in the U.S., author of *The Rise and Fall of the Great Powers*, said, "Of all the civilizations of the pre-modern period, none was as well-developed or as progressive as that of China."

Foreigners who came to China were often astonished at what they saw and heard. The Greek geographer Pausanias in the second century A.D. gave the first account in the West of the technique of silk production in China: "The Chinese feed a spider-like insect with millet and reeds. After five years the insect's stomach splits open, and silk is extracted therefrom." From this extract, we can see that the Europeans at that time did not know the art of silk manufacture. In the middle of the 9th century A.D., an Arabian writer includes the following anecdote in his *Account of China and India*:

"One day, an Arabian merchant called upon the military governor of Guangzhou. Throughout the meeting, the visitor could not keep his eyes off the governor's chest. Noticing this, the latter asked the Arab merchant what he was staring at. The merchant replied, 'Through the silk robe you are wearing, I can faintly see a black mole on your chest. Your robe must be made out of very fine silk indeed!' The governor burst out laughing, and holding out his sleeve invited the merchant to count how many garments he was wearing. The merchant did so, and discovered that the governor was actually wearing five silk robes, one on top of the other, and they were made of such fine material that a tiny mole could be seen through them all! Moreover, the governor explained that the robes he was wearing were not made of the finest silk at all; silk of the highest grade was reserved for the garments worn by the provincial governor."

The references to tea in this book (the author calls it "dried grass") reveal that the custom of drinking tea was unknown in the Arab countries at that time: "The king of China's revenue comes mainly from taxes on salt and the dry leaves of a kind of grass which is drunk after boiled water is poured on it. This dried grass is sold at a high price in every city in the country. The Chinese call it 'cha.' The bush is like alfalfa, except that it bears more leaves, which are also more fragrant than alfalfa. It has a slightly bitter taste, and when it is infused in boiling water it is said to have medicinal properties."

Foreign visitors showed especial admiration for Chinese medicine. One wrote, "China has very good medical conditions. Poor people are given money to buy medicines by the government."

In this period, when Chinese culture was in full bloom, scholars flocked from all over the world to China for sightseeing and for study. Chang'an, the capital of the Tang Dynasty was host to visitors from as far away as the Byzantine Empire, not to mention the neighboring countries of Asia. Chang'an, at that time the world's greatest metropolis, was packed with thousands of foreign dignitaries, students, diplomats, merchants, artisans and entertainers. Japan especially sent contingent after contingent of envoys to the Tang court. Worthy of note are the accounts of life in Chang'an written by Abeno Nakamaro, a Japanese scholar who studied in China and had close friendships with ministers of the Tang court and many Chinese scholars in a period of over 50 years. The description throws light on the exchanges between Chinese and foreigners in this period. When Abeno was supposedly lost at sea on his way back home, the leading poet of the time, Li Bai, wrote a eulogy for him.

The following centuries saw a steady increase in the accounts of China written by Western visitors. The Italian Marco Polo described conditions in China during the Yuan Dynasty in his *Travels*. However, until advances in the science of navigation led to the opening of east-west shipping routes at the beginning of the 16th century Sino-Western cultural exchanges were coloured by fantasy and conjecture. Concrete progress was made when a contingent of religious missionaries, men well versed in Western science and technology, made their way to China, ushering in an era of direct contacts between China and the West. The experience of this era was embodied in the career of the Italian Jesuit Matteo Ricci. Arriving in China in 1582, Ricci died in Beijing in 1610. Apart from his missionary work, Ricci accomplished two historically symbolic tasks — one was the translation into Latin of the "Four Books," together with annotations, in 1594; the other was the translation into Chinese of Euclid's *Elements*.

The rough translations of the "Four Books" and other Chinese classical works by Western missionaries, and the publication of Père du Halde's *Description Geographique, Historique, Chronologique, Politique, et Physique de l'Empire de la Chine* revealed an exotic culture to Western readers, and sparked a "China fever," during which the eyes of many Western intellectuals were fixed on China. Some of these intellectuals, including Leibniz, held China in high esteem; others, such as Hegel, nursed a critical attitude toward Chinese culture. Leibniz considered that some aspects of Chinese thought were close to his own views, such as the philosophy of the *Book of Changes* and his own binary system. Hegel, on the other hand, as mentioned above, considered that China had developed no proper philosophy of its own. Nevertheless, no matter whether the reaction was one of admiration, criticism, acceptance or rejection, Sino-Western exchanges were of great significance. The transmission of advanced Chinese science and technology to the West, especially the Chinese inventions of paper-making, gunpowder, printing and the compass, greatly changed the face of the whole world. Karl Marx said, "Chinese gunpowder blew the feudal class of knights to smithereens; the compass opened up world markets and built colonies; and printing became an implement of Protestantism and the most powerful lever and necessary precondition for intellectual development and creation." The English philosopher Roger Bacon said that China's four great inventions had "changed the face of the whole world and the state of affairs of everything."

3

Ancient China gave birth to a large number of eminent scientists, such as Zu Chongzhi, Li Shizhen, Sun Simiao, Zhang Heng, Shen Kuo and Bi

Sheng. They produced numerous treatises on scientific subjects, including *The Manual of Important Arts for the People's Welfare, Nine Chapters on the Mathematical Art, A Treatise on Febrile Diseases* and *Compendium of Materia Medica*. Their accomplishments included ones whose influence has been felt right down to modern times, such as the armillary sphere, seismograph, Dujiangyan water conservancy project, Dunhuang Grottoes, Grand Canal and Great Wall. But from the latter part of the 15th century, and for the next 400 years, Europe gradually became the cultural centre upon which the world's eyes were fixed. The world's most outstanding scientists then were England's Isaac Newton, Poland's Copernicus, France's Marie Curie, Germany's Rontgen and Einstein, Italy's Galileo, Russia's Mendelev and America's Edison.

The Chinese people then began to think: What is the cause of the rise and fall of nations? Moreover, how did it happen that gunpowder, invented in China and transmitted to the West, in no time at all made Europe powerful enough to batter down the gates of China herself?

It took the Opium War to wake China from its reverie. The first generation to make the bold step of "turning our eyes once again to the rest of the world" was represented by Lin Zexu and Wei Yuan. Zeng Guofan and Li Hongzhang started the Westernization Movement, and later intellectuals raised the slogan of "Democracy and Science." Noble-minded patriots, realizing that China had fallen behind in the race for modernization, set out on a painful quest. But in backwardness lay the motivation for change, and the quest produced the embryo of a towering hope, and the Chinese people finally gathered under a banner proclaiming a "March Toward Science."

On the threshold of the 21st century, the world is moving in the direction of becoming an integrated entity. This trend is becoming clearer by the day. In fact, the history of the various peoples of the world is also becoming the history of mankind as a whole. Today, it is impossible for any nation's culture to develop without absorbing the excellent aspects of the cultures of other peoples. When Western culture absorbs aspects of Chinese culture, this is not just because it has come into contact with Chinese culture, but also because of the active creativity and development of Western culture itself; and vice versa. The various cultures of the world's peoples are a precious heritage which we all share. Mankind no longer lives on different continents, but on one big continent, or in a "global village." And so, in this era characterized by an all-encompassing network of knowledge and information we should learn from each other and march in step along the highway of development to construct a brand-new "global village."

Western learning is still being transmitted to the East, and vice versa. China is accelerating its pace of absorption of the best parts of the cultures of other countries, and there is no doubt that both the West and the East need the nourishment of Chinese culture. Based on this recognition, we have edited and published the *Library of Chinese Classics* in a Chinese-English format as an introduction to the corpus of traditional Chinese culture in a comprehensive and systematic translation. Through this collection, our aim is to reveal to the world the aspirations and dreams of the Chinese people over the past 5,000 years and the splendour of the new historical era in China. Like a phoenix rising from the ashes, the Chinese people in unison are welcoming the cultural sunrise of the new century.

August 1999

序

袁行霈

　　中国是一个诗的国度，诗的历史源远流长，在社会生活中发挥着重要的作用。早在先秦时代，孔子就说过："不学诗，无以言。"唐代开始以诗取士，读诗作诗更成为儿童必修的内容。适应这种需要，早已出现了诗歌的启蒙读物。宋代刘克庄曾编过一部《分门纂类唐代时贤千家诗选》二十二卷，选录唐宋诗人565家的作品1281首，影响较大。但是其中多有错谬，又往往把律诗截去半首改作绝句，再加上篇幅浩繁，不便于儿童学习。此书流传到明清，坊间又刻有多种《千家诗》，沿用其书名，而重新加以编排，篇幅也减少了许多。其中流传最广的是明清之间王相的选注本，选录诗歌223首，按七言绝句、七言律诗、五言绝句、五言律诗的顺序编排，每种体裁之下再按春夏秋冬四季为序，除唐宋诗人外，增补了明朝的个别作品。王相选注本《千家诗》虽有通俗易懂、便于记诵的优点，但毕竟是适应当时的需要而编选的，其中很多内容已不适合今天的读者，编排方法也有局限。

　　为了弘扬祖国优秀的传统文化，对少年儿童进行爱国主义教育，培养他们高尚的道德情操和审美趣味，启迪他们的人生智慧，我们编选了这部书，取名《新编千家诗》。我们保存原来流行本《千家诗》的优点，而又力求有一种新的适应我们这个时代的面貌。我们注意选取那些寓意深刻、情调健康、意境开阔、形象鲜明、脍炙人口的作品。选诗的范围仍以唐宋两代的近体诗为主，但又不限于此。从时代上讲，增加了汉魏六朝以及元明清直到近代的作品；从体裁上讲，增加了五七言古诗。所选诗歌共152首，为了便于儿童由浅入深地诵习，按五言绝句、七言绝句、五言律诗、七言律诗、五言古诗、七言古诗这种顺序编排，同一体裁下则按诗人时代先后排列。

《新编千家诗》是一本十分通俗的古典诗歌阅读本，但我们并不因此而采取轻率的态度。相反地，正因为面向广大的读者，特别是少年儿童，我们感到责任格外重大。在走向现代化的进程中，我们希望少年儿童从古典诗词中多吸取一些营养，成长得更加茁壮；而不要断了祖国传统文化的乳汁，忘了自己赖以生存的根。我曾向欣然与我合作的朋友们说："这是一件积德的事。"正是基于这种考虑，我们暂时放下自己的学术研究，热情地投入了这项工作。

《新编千家诗》出版以后得到众多读者的喜爱，成为许多家长教孩子学习和背诵古典诗歌的读本，一版再版，发行了多次，我和我的合作者们深感欣慰。《大中华文库》决定收入这部《新编千家诗》，配以徐放先生的白话翻译和许渊冲先生的英文翻译，使此书文白对照、中西合璧，实在是一件值得高兴的事。

徐放先生是一位热情洋溢的新诗人，对中国古典诗歌也做过系统研究，上世纪80年代以来陆续出版了《唐诗今译》、《杜甫诗今译》、《宋诗今译》、《陆游诗今译》、《唐宋词今译》等书。他采用自由诗的形式，在深入理解原作的基础上，用白话表达原作的思想感情和风格，为古典诗词的通俗化和普及化作出了贡献。

北京大学著名教授许渊冲先生还将此书译为英文,在国内外发行。许渊冲先生(1921—),笔名X.Y.Z,江西南昌人,1943年毕业于清华大学外文系,1944年入清华大学外国文学研究所学习,后赴欧留学。回国后在北京等地外国语学院任英文、法文教授。他在国内外出版了中、英、法文的文学作品五十余部,尤致力于把中国文化精粹推向世界,为中国文化走向世界开辟道路。他翻译过《诗经》、《楚辞》、《汉魏六朝诗150首》、《唐诗三百首》、《宋词三百首》、《李白诗选》、《苏东坡诗词选》、《西厢记》、《元明清诗》等十余种书。他的《新编千家诗》英译本,以流畅优美而又琅琅上口的英语准确地传达出中国古典诗歌丰富的涵义和独特的神韵,无异于一次美的再创造。我曾有幸跟许先生为邻,也曾跟他讨论过中国古典诗歌的英译问题,在讨论中间他时常情不自禁地朗诵起他所译的古诗,让我听得入迷。有了他的翻译,《新编千家诗》犹如添了翅膀,可以飞向世界各地的读者中间。这是此书的幸事,也是李白、杜甫等古代诗人的幸事。

Preface

China is a country of poetry. Chinese poetry has a long history, and has played an important role in Chinese society. As early as the pre-Qin era, Confucius stated that "if one has not studied poetry, he is not worthy of my conversation." During the Tang dynasty the govemment used poetry as a means of selecting state officials. Since then, reading and writing poetry became an indispensable part of a child's education. Several anthologies were published to meet this demand. Liu Kezhuang of the Song dynasty once compiled *The Categorized Anthology of Poems by a Thousand Great Tang Poets*. It consisted of 22 volumes, and altogether selected 1,281 poems by 565 poets. Although this anthology had great influences, it nevertheless contained many mistakes. For example, it often cut out half of a regulated verse and categorized it as a quatrain. Moreover, it was too long and cumbersome for teaching children. Later, during the Ming and Qing dynasties, there appeared many different and much shorter editions of *Poems by a Thousand Poets*. The most famous of these was one edited by Wang Xiang. It selected 223 poems and divided them into heptasyllabic quatrains, heptasyllabic regulated poems, pentasyllabic quatrains, and pentasyllabic regulated poems. Under each form, the poems were arranged according to the seasonal sequence, namely Spring, Summer, Autumn, and Winter. In addition to the poems by Tang and Song dynasties poets, Wang Xiang's edition also added a few pieces by Ming dynasty poets. Although Wang Xiang's edition was simple to read and easy to memorize, it nonetheless was compiled for the need of his time. Therefore, it is no longer appropriate for today's audience, not to mention the fact that it had itslimitations in its format.

The purpose of compiling this *Gems of Classical Chinese Poetry* is to glorify the cultural tradition of our nation, to teach our youth to be patriotic, to instill in them high morality and aesthetic sensitivity, and to stimulate their search for wisdom. We have retained many merits of the old editions, but also aimed to make this new edition serve the needs of a new era. In selecting the poems, we have given our preferences to those that are profound, healthy, with broad scope and vivid images. The poems selected are mostly the recent-style poems of Tang and Song dynasties, but not limited to them. In time periods, we have added some poems from the Han, Wei, Jin, Northern and Southern dynasties, as well as works from the Ming-Qing dynasties to modern era. In poetic styles, we have added some pentasyllabic and heptasyllabic ancient-style poems. This new edition contains 152 poems. To make it easy for children to read and memorize, we have arranged the poems in the order of pentasyllabic quatrains, heptasyllabic quatrains, pentasyllabic regulated verses, heptasyllabic regulated verses, pentasyllabic ancient-style poems, and heptasyllabic ancient-style poems. Under each form, the poets are arranged in a chronological order.

Although this *Gems of Classical Chinese Poetry* is a popular anthology of classical poetry, we have not taken it lightly. Quite the contrary, precisely because it is intended for the general audience, especially for children and youth, we have felt a special responsibility. In our march to modernization, we hope that our children and youth will be nourished by classical poetry, so that they may thrive even more. We hope that they will not find themselves uprooted from their cultural origin. I once said to friends who were cooperating with me in this endeavor, that this was "an act of virtue." It was out of this consideration that we temporarily put aside our academic research and devoted ourselves to this work.

Since its publication, the *Gems of Classical Chinese Poetry* has become a favorite for many readers. It has become a classical-poetry text for many parents and their children. For this mason, it has been printed a number of times. My co-editors and I find a great deal of consolation in this. Now, the Zhonghua Book Company wishes to include this book in the *Library of Chinese Classics series*. Mr. Xu Fang has translated the original text into modem Chinese, and Mr. Xu Yuan Zhong has translated the poems into English. I am delighted that we now can offer readers a book that contains both the original poems and their modem Chinese and English transtations.

Mr. Xu Fang is an energetic poet of new-style poetry. He is also well versed in classical poetry, and has published several modem Chinese translations of classical poetry, such as *A Modern Chinese Translation of Tang Dynasty Poems, A Modern Chinese Translation of Du Fu's Poems, A Modern Chinese Translation of Song Dynasty Poems, A Modern Chinese Translation of Lu You's Poems,* and *A Modern Chinese Translation of Song Lyrics of the Tang and Song Dynasties.* His free-verse translations are based on his deep understanding of the original poems. They express in modem Chinese the feelings, thoughts and styles of the original texts. They have made classical poetry more accessible to the general audience.

Mr. Xu Yuan Zhong, a renowned professor at Peking University, has translated these poems into English. Mr. Xu, whose pen-name is X. Y. Z., is a native of Nanchang, Jiangxi province. He graduated from the Department of Foreign Languages and Literature of Tsinghua University in 1943. A year later he was accepted into the Institute of Foreign Literature at Tsinghua. Later he went to study in Europe.since his return, he has taught English and French at many universities and colleges in Beijing and other places. He has published more than 50 books and translations about Chinese literature, English literature, and French literature. He has particularly dedicated himself to introducing Chinese culture to the world. His numerous translations include *The Book of Poetry, Elegies of the South, 150 Poems of the Han、the Wei and the Six Dynasties, 300 Tang Poems, 300 Song Poems, Selected Poems of Li Bai, Selected Poems of Su Dongpo, Romance of the Western Bower, and Poems of the Yuan、Ming and Qing Dynasties.* His translation of the *Gems of Classical Chinese Poetry* recreates in rhythmic English the rich meaning and unique spirit of classical Chinese poetry. It is lucid, beautiful, and accurate. I have had the honor of having him as my neighbor, and have discussed with him issues in translating Chinese poetry into English. Often, he would recite his fascinating translations to me. Now, his translation has added wings to the *Gems of classical Chinese Poetry.* With these wings it will be able to fly to the readers all over the world. This is an honor both for this book, and for Li Bai, Du Fu, and other ancient poets.

Translated by Wu Fusheng

译　序

许渊冲

21世纪是全球化的世纪。新世纪的新人不但应该了解全球的文化，还应该使本国文化走向世界，成为全球文化的一部分，使世界文化更加灿烂辉煌。

近来我国电视播放了小学生背诵唐诗英译文的情况，我想，这是我国文化走向世界的一个新开端。其实，外国来宾引用中国诗词早有先例：如美国总统尼克松访华时，引用过"一万年太久，只争朝夕"的词句；里根总统引用了"海内存知己，天涯若比邻"的名言。可见中国诗词已经可以说是全球文化的一部分了。

因此，中华书局约我翻译《新编千家诗》时，我很高兴接受这个任务。因为中国人英译的《楚辞》，美国有个学者说是"当算英美文学里的一座高峰"；英国智慧女神出版社认为中国人英译的《西厢记》可和莎士比亚的作品相媲美。所以我希望《新编千家诗》英译本的出版，对我国的文化走向世界，也可以作出新的贡献。

但是，诗无达诂，在译成英文时，我就要看哪种理解更符合古诗本意，更好翻译，再采用哪种解释。总的说来，我认为译诗是一种再创作，等于原诗作者用译语的创作，译者要尽可能发挥译语优势，要尽可能传达原诗的意美、音美、形美，可以采用等化、浅化、深化的方法。如"白日依山尽，黄河入海流",基本上是等化的英译;"欲穷千里目,更上一层楼",基本上是用浅化的方法,因为"千里"并不真是九百九十九加一里,所以可浅化为登高望远的意思;至于深化,王维《鸟鸣涧》的"人闲桂花落,……时鸣春涧中","桂花落"一般说是秋天,怎么说"春涧"呢?我译成使涧充满了春意,这就可以说是深化了。等化、浅化、深化都是为了传达原诗的意美;押韵是传达原诗的音美;一个中文字大致译成英文两个音节,这是传达原诗的形美。意美、音美、形美是我提出的译诗"三美论";"三化"是译诗的方法论;目的是使读者知之、好之、乐之,"三之"是译诗的目的论。

  如果译诗能使中国读者理解原作,那就是"知之";如果能使人喜欢,那就是"好之";能使人愉快,那就是"乐之"。如果能使英美读者知之、好之、乐之,那就是使中国文学走向世界。如果英美读者能把译诗当成英美文学高峰,认为译诗可和英美诗人媲美,那中国文学就丰富了全球文化。

  如果21世纪的中国学生不但能背诵中文诗词,还能背诵诗词的英译文,那语文水平、文化水平,不都是大大提高了吗?不是向21世纪的全球化迈进了一大步吗?如果英美学生不但能理解中国诗文,还能欣赏甚至背诵诗词译文,那不也是向全球化迈进了吗?

  20世纪科学技术突飞猛进,超过了以前19个世纪,但思想文化水平有没有同样突飞猛进呢?恐怕落后得多吧!而这正是20世纪最大的悲剧。希望这本小书的出版,对21世纪全球文化的建设,能够添上一砖一瓦!希望新世纪的新人能享受到更加和平、更加繁荣、更加幸福的生活!

Preface

X. Y. Z.

It is said that the 21st century will be an age of globalization. The new generation worthy of the new age should be bred not only in its national culture but also in the global culture or that of the whole world. Therefore, each nation should try to globalize its own culture,in other words,to make its culture known to the world and become a part of global culture.

Recently Chinese pupils in some primary schools have begun to recite classical Chinese verse not only in the original but also in its English translation. I think this is,in one respect,the beginning of the globalization of Chinese culture. In fact,foreign guests visiting China have already cited classical Chinese verse in their addresses. For instance,President Nixon of the United States quoted the following verse of Mao Zedong:

> So many deeds
> Bear no delay.
> Sun and earth turn;
> Time flies away.
> Ten thousand years are too long.
> Seize but the day!

And President Reagan cited the following couplet of Wang Bo:

> If you have friends who know your heart,
> Distance cannot keep you apart.

This shows a part of Chinese poetry has already become a part of global culture.

As my English version of *Elegies of the South* composed in the third century B.C. is considered by Jon Kowallis of Melbourne University as a high peak even in English and American literature,and Minerva Press says my English version of *Romance of the Western Bower* vies with Shakespeare's

Romeo and Juliet in appeal and artistry, I venture to expect that *Gems of Classical Chinese Poetry* may also contribute to the globalization of Chinese culture.

As classical Chinese poetry has no generally accepted interpretation, I just try to make the fullest possible use of the best expressions in the target language, for the original is the best words in the best order in the source language, as said an English poet of the 19th century. I think verse translation is a creative or recreative work, for the original is a creative work, so a translator should recreate in the target language what the author of the original creates in the source language. In other words, a translator should be the author metamorphosed into a foreign poet.

My principle of verse translation is to make the translated verse faithful and beautiful, as beautiful as the original in sense, in sound and in form. The methods I use are equalization, generalization and particularization. We may compare the examples given below.

1. (word-for-word translation):
   yellow   river   enter   sea   flow
2. (equalization): The Yellow River seawards flows.
3. (word-for-word translation):
   desire   exhaust   thousand   mile   view
   more   ascend   one   floor   tower
4. (generalization): You will enjoy a grander sight
              By climbing to a greater height.
  (Here the view over a thousand miles is generalized into a grander
   sight and one floor more into a greater height.)
5. (word-for-word translation):
   often   sing   spring   dale   in
6. (particularization):
   Their fitful twitters fill the dale with spring.
      (Here "often" is particularized into "fitful", "sing" into "twitters"
      and "in spring dale" into "fill the dale with spring".)

Equalization, generalization and particularization may serve to make the English version read as beautiful as the original in sense. Rhythm and rhyme serve to make it read beautiful in sound. Heroic couplets and alexandrines are used to preserve the original beauty in form. These methods intend to make the reader understand,enjoy and delight in the English version as a Chinese reader in the original. If foreign readers can understand,appreciate and delight as Chinese readers do,then the English version of Chinese verse may be said to have become a part of global literature. If they happen to consider the version as high peaks in foreign literature or the Chinese poets as rivals with foreign poets,then Chinese poetry may be said to have enriched global culture.

If Chinese students can recite classical verse not only in Chinese but also in English,then they may be said to have raised their cultural level and made a big stride toward the globalization of the new age. If foreign students can appreciate and recite not only their own literature but also Chinese poetry in English translation,can we not say that the world has made a big stride toward globalization?

In the 20th century science and technology made far greater progress than culture and ideology,which may be said to have lagged far behind. This imbalance between science and culture(in a narrow sense)may be said to be one of the causes of the tragedy of the 20th century. Therefore,I wish the publication of *Gems of Classical Chinese Poetry* may make a new contribution to the world's cultural globalization. I also wish the new generation may enjoy a more peaceful,more prosperous and far happier life than our generation of the 20th century.

目录

登鹳雀楼　王之涣	2
春晓　孟浩然	4
长干曲其一　崔颢	6
长干曲其二　崔颢	8
鸟鸣涧　王维	10
杂诗其二　王维	12
相思　王维	14
静夜思　李白	16
秋浦歌其十五　李白	18
独坐敬亭山　李白	20
逢雪宿芙蓉山主人　刘长卿	22
问刘十九　白居易	24
悯农其一　李绅	26
悯农其二　李绅	28
江雪　柳宗元	30
寻隐者不遇　贾岛	32
乐游原　李商隐	34
江上渔者　范仲淹	36
陶者　梅尧臣	38
晚过水北　欧阳修	40
江上　王安石	42
乌江　李清照	44

Contents

On the Stork Tower Wang Zhihuan	3
Spring Morning Meng Haoran	5
Songs on the River I Cui Hao	7
Songs on the River II Cui Hao	9
The Dale of Singing Birds Wang Wei	11
Our Native Place Wang Wei	13
Love Seeds Wang Wei	15
Thoughts on a Still Night Li Bai	17
My White Hair Li Bai	19
Sitting Alone in Face of Mount Jingting Li Bai	21
Seeking Shelter in Lotus Hill on a Snowy Night Liu Changqing	23
An Invitation Bai Juyi	25
The Peasants I Li Shen	27
The Peasants II Li Shen	29
Snow on the River Liu Zongyuan	31
For an Absent Recluse Jia Dao	33
On the Plain of Tombs Li Shangyin	35
The Fisherman on the River Fan Zhongyan	37
The Tile-Maker Mei Yaochen	39
Passing by the Northern Shore at Dusk Ouyang Xiu	41
On the River Wang Anshi	43
The Black River Li Qingzhao	45

咏雪其一　傅察	46
灯花　王质	48
客晓　沈受宏	50
舟中夜书所见　查慎行	52
苔　袁枚	54

咏柳　贺知章	56
回乡偶书其一　贺知章	58
出塞其一　王昌龄	60
芙蓉楼送辛渐　王昌龄	62

| 九月九日忆山东兄弟　王维 | 64 |

送元二使安西　王维	66
送沈子福归江东　王维	68
黄鹤楼送孟浩然之广陵　李白	70

望天门山　李白	72
赠汪伦　李白	74
早发白帝城　李白	76
别董大　高适	78
绝句四首其三　杜甫	80
枫桥夜泊　张继	82
夜月　刘方平	84
滁州西涧　韦应物	86
早春呈水部张十八员外其一　韩愈	88
竹枝词其一　刘禹锡	90

Snow I Fu Cha	47
Blooming Flame Wang Zhi	49
At Dawn Shen Shouhong	51
A Night Scene Viewed from a Boat Zha Shenxing	53
Moss Yuan Mei	55
The Willow He Zhizhang	57
Home Coming I He Zhizhang	59
On the Frontier I Wang Changling	61
Farewell to Xin Jian at Lotus Tower Wang Changling	63
Thinking of My Brothers on Mountain-Climbing Day Wang Wei	65
A Farewell Song Wang Wei	67
Seeing a Friend Off to the East Wang Wei	69
Seeing Meng Haoran Off at Yellow Crane Tower Li Bai	71
Mount Heaven's Gate Viewd from Afar Li Bai	73
To Wang Lun Li Bai	75
Leaving White Emperor Town at Dawn Li Bai	77
Farewell to a Lutist Gao Shi	79
A Quatrain Du Fu	81
Mooring by Maple Bridge at Night Zhang Ji	83
A Moonlit Night Liu Fangping	85
On the West Stream at Chuzhou Wei Yingwu	87
Early Spring Written for Secretary Zhang Ji I Han Yu	89
Bamboo Branch Song Liu Yuxi	91

望洞庭　刘禹锡	92
暮江吟　白居易	94
秋夕　杜牧	96
山行　杜牧	98
清明　杜牧	100
夜雨寄北　李商隐	102
登飞来峰　王安石	104
泊船瓜洲　王安石	106
北陂杏花　王安石	108
春日偶成　程颢	110
六月二十七日望湖楼醉书其一　苏轼	112
饮湖上初晴后雨其二　苏轼	114
题西林壁　苏轼	116
惠崇春江晓景　苏轼	118
初见嵩山　张耒	120
春游湖　徐俯	122
病牛　李纲	124
晓出净慈送林子方　杨万里	126
闲居初夏午睡起其一　杨万里	128
过松源晨炊漆公店　杨万里	130
秋夜将晓出篱门迎凉有感其二　陆游	132

Lake Dongting Viewed from Afar	Liu Yuxi	93
Sunset and Moonrise on the River	Bai Juyi	95
An Autumn Night	Du Mu	97
Going Uphill	Du Mu	99
The Mourning Day	Du Mu	101
Written on a Rainy Night to a Friend in the North Li Shangyin		103
On the Winged Peak	Wang Anshi	105
Moored at the Ferry	Wang Anshi	107
Poolside Apricot Flowers	Wang Anshi	109
Impromptu Lines on a Spring Day	Cheng Hao	111
Written While Drunken in Lake View Pavilion I Su Shi		113
Drinking at the Lake First in Sunny, Then in Rainy, Weather II Su Shi		115
Written on the Wall of West Forest Temple Su Shi		117
Vernal Scene on a River	Su Shi	119
At First Sight of Mount Song	Zhang Lei	121
A Spring Day on the Lake	Xu Fu	123
To a Sick Buffalo	Li Gang	125
The Lakeside Temple at Dawn	Yang Wanli	127
Rising After a Siesta in Early Summer Yang Wanli		129
Passing by Songyuan	Yang Wanli	131
Early Dawn at My Wicket Gate	Lu You	133

十一月四日风雨大作　陆游	134
梅花绝句　陆游	136
示儿　陆游	138
四时田园杂兴其四十四　范成大	140
横塘　范成大	142
春日　朱熹	144
水口行舟其一　朱熹	146
观书有感　朱熹	148
题临安邸　林升	150
约客　赵师秀	152
乡村四月　翁卷	154
寒夜　杜耒	156
村晚　雷震	158
游园不值　叶绍翁	160
春暮游小园　王淇	162
溪桥晚兴　郑协	164
溪上　刘因	166
白梅　王冕	168
墨梅　王冕	170
海乡竹枝词其一　杨维桢	172
石灰吟　于谦	174
夏口夜泊别友人　李梦阳	176
竹枝词其四　袁宏道	178
真州绝句其四　王士祯	180

The Storm on the Fourth Day of the Eleventh Moon

   Lu You   135

A Quatrain on Mume Blossoms Lu You   137

Testament to My Sons   Lu You   139

Rural Life in Autumn   Fan Chengda   141

The Lakeside Lane   Fan Chengda   143

A Spring Day   Zhu Xi   145

Boating After a Stormy Night   Zhu Xi   147

The Book   Zhu Xi   149

Written in the New Capital   Lin Sheng   151

A Promise Broken   Zhao Shixiu   153

The Countryside in the Fourth Moon   Weng Juan 155

A Cold Night   Du Lei   157

A Village at Dusk   Lei Zhen   159

A Closed Garden   Ye Shaoweng   161

Late Spring in a Garden   Wang Qi   163

One Evening on a Bridge over the Brook

    Zheng Xie   165

On the Brook   Liu Yin   167

The White Mume Blossoms   Wang Mian   169

Mume Blossoms Painted in Black Ink   Wang Mian 171

A Seaside Bamboo Branch Song   Yang Weizhen 173

Song of the Lime   Yu Qian   175

Farewell to a Friend at Yellow Crane Tower

    Li Mengyang   177

Bamboo Branch Song   Yuan Hongdao   179

A Quatrain on the Northern Shore   Wang Shizhen 181

蒙阴　厉鹗	182
竹石　郑燮	184
新雷　张维屏	186
己亥杂诗其五　龚自珍	188
己亥杂诗其一百二十五　龚自珍	190
狱中题壁　谭嗣同	192
送杜少府之任蜀州　王勃	194
望月怀远　张九龄	196
过故人庄　孟浩然	198
次北固山下　王湾	200
使至塞上　王维	202
汉江临眺　王维	204
终南山　王维	206
渡荆门送别　李白	208
秋登宣城谢脁北楼　李白	210
送友人　李白	212
月夜　杜甫	214
春望　杜甫	216
月夜忆舍弟　杜甫	218
春夜喜雨　杜甫	220
喜见外弟又言别　李益	222
赋得古原草送别　白居易	224

Mount Meng Li E	183
Bamboo in the Rock Zheng Xie	185
The First Thunder Zhang Weiping	187
Miscellanies of the Year 1839 V Gong Zizhen	189
Miscellenies of the Year 1839 Gong Zizhen	191
Written on the Wall of the Prison Tan Sitong	193
Farewell to Prefect Du Wang Bo	195
Looking at the Moon and Longing for One Far Away Zhang Jiuling	197
Visiting an Old Friend Meng Haoran	199
Passing by Beigu Mountain Wang Wan	201
On Mission to the Frontier Wang Wei	203
A View of the Han River Wang Wei	205
Mount Eternal South Wang Wei	207
Beyond Mount Thorn-gate Li Bai	209
On the Northern Tower of Xie Tiao at Xuancheng in Autumn Li Bai	211
Farewell to a Friend Li Bai	213
A Moonlit Night Du Fu	215
Spring View Du Fu	217
Thinking of My Brothers on a Moonlit Night Du Fu	219
Happy Rain on a Spring Night Du Fu	221
Meeting and Parting with My Cousin Li Yi	223
Grass on the Ancient Plain-Farewell to a Friend Bai Juyi	225

题扬州禅智寺　杜牧	226
晚晴　李商隐	228
商山早行　温庭筠	230
鲁山山行　梅尧臣	232
游大林　周敦颐	234
雨过　周紫芝	236
白菊　许廷镣	238
黄鹤楼　崔颢	240
闻官军收河南河北　杜甫	242
江村　杜甫	244
蜀相　杜甫	246
左迁至蓝关示侄孙湘　韩愈	248
酬乐天扬州初逢席上见赠　刘禹锡	250
钱塘湖春行　白居易	252
无题　李商隐	254
山中寡妇　杜荀鹤	256
贫女　秦韬玉	258
戏答元珍　欧阳修	260
偶成　程颢	262
游山西村　陆游	264
书愤　陆游	266
临安春雨初霁　陆游	268

The West Bamboo Temple at Yangzhou	Du Mu	227
A Sunny Evening after Rain	Li Shangyin	229
Early Departure	Wen Tingyun	231
Roving in the Mountains of Dew	Mei Yaochen	233
Visiting Dalin Temple	Zhou Dunyi	235
After Rain	Zhou Zizhi	237
To White Chrysanthemums	Xu Tingheng	239
Yellow Crane Tower	Cui Hao	241
Recapture of the Regions North and South of the Yellow River	Du Fu	243
The Riverside Village	Du Fu	245
The Premier of Shu	Du Fu	247
Written for My Grandnephew at the Blue Pass	Han Yu	249
Reply to Bai Juyi Whom I Met for the First Time at a Banquet in Yangzhou	Liu Yuxi	251
Lake Qiantang in Spring	Bai Juyi	253
To One Unnamed	Li Shangyin	255
A Widow Living in the Mountain	Du Xunhe	257
A Poor Maid	Qin Taoyu	259
Reply to Yuan Zhen	Ouyang Xiu	261
A Random Poem	Cheng Hao	263
The Western Mountain Village	Lu You	265
Indignation	Lu You	267
A Sunny Spring Day after a Rainy Night in the Capital	Lu You	269

过零丁洋　文天祥　　　　　　270
赴戍登程口占示家人　林则徐　　272
黄海舟中日人索句并见日俄战争
　　地图　秋瑾　　　　　　　274

江南　汉乐府　　　　　　　　276
长歌行　汉乐府　　　　　　　278
赠从弟其二　刘桢　　　　　　280
野田黄雀行　曹植　　　　　　282
归园田居其三　陶渊明　　　　284
宿五松山下荀媪家　李白　　　286

望岳　杜甫　　　　　　　　　288
游子吟　孟郊　　　　　　　　290

敕勒歌　北朝民歌　　　　　　292
春江花月夜　张若虚　　　　　294
行路难其一　李白　　　　　　300

茅屋为秋风所破歌　杜甫　　　302
白雪歌送武判官归京　岑参　　306
琵琶行　白居易　　　　　　　310
渔翁　柳宗元　　　　　　　　320

The Lonely Ocean Wen Tianxiang	271
Before Going into Exile Lin Zexu	273
Lines Written at the Request of a Japanese in a Ship on the Yellow Sea after Seeing a Map of the Russo-Japanese War Qiu Jin	275
The Southern Rivershore Music Bureau	277
A Slow Song Music Bureau	279
To My Cousin Liu Zhen	281
Song of the Yellow Bird Cao Zhi	283
Return to Nature Tao Yuanming	285
Passing One Night in an Old Woman's Hut at the Foot of Mount Five Pines Li Bai	287
Gazing on Mount Tai Du Fu	289
Song of the Parting Son Meng Jiao	291
A Shepherd's Song Anonymous	293
A Moonlit Night on the Spring River Zhang Ruoxu	295
Hard Is the Way Li Bai	301
My Cottage Unroofed by Autumn Gale Du Fu	303
Song of White Snow in Farewell to Secretary Wu Going Back to the Capital Cen Shen	307
Song of a *Pipa* Player Bai Juyi	311
A Fisherman Liu Zongyuan	321

登 鹳 雀 楼

王之涣

白日依山尽，
黄河入海流。
欲穷千里目，
更上一层楼。

今译

白日依傍着西山
已经落下，
滔滔黄河
正向着东海在奔流。
要想看清
千里以外的所在，
就得登上——
更高的那一层城楼。

ON THE STORK TOWER

Wang Zhihuan

The sun along the mountain bows,

The Yellow River seawards flows.

You will enjoy a grander sight

By climbing to a greater height.

春 晓

孟浩然

春眠不觉晓，
处处闻啼鸟。
夜来风雨声，
花落知多少！

今译

春睡晚起啦
当听到处处是鸟啼的时候
才知道天已破晓。
呵
昨夜里，曾经有风雨之声，
那些花儿
也不知道被打伤吹落了多少？

SPRING MORNING

Meng Haoran

This morn of spring in bed I'm lying,

Not to awake till birds are crying.

After one night of winds and showers,

How many are the fallen flowers!

长 干 曲

崔 颢

其 一

君家何处住？
妾住在横塘。
停船暂借问，
或恐是同乡。

今 译

你的家
住在何处？
我的家
住在横塘。
停下船来，
暂且发问，
我们两个
也许还是同乡！

SONGS ON THE RIVER

Cui Hao

I THE WOMAN'S SONG

" Where are you coming from?

On the shore I've my home.

Will you rest on your oar?

Are we from the same shore? "

长干曲

崔颢

其 二

家临九江水，
来去九江侧。
同是长干人，
自小不相识。

今译

我的家，
住在九江汇集的长江边上，
天天都来来去去在——
这九江汇集的长江之侧。
我们本来都是——
长干里的人，
可是
自小以来
却互不认识！

SONGS ON THE RIVER

Cui Hao

II THE MAN'S SONG

" I dwell by riverside;

I sail on river wide.

We live on the same shore,

Not knowing it before. "

鸟 鸣 涧

王 维

人闲桂花落,
夜静春山空。
月出惊山鸟,
时鸣春涧中。

今译

人闲着
看桂花在飘落,
夜,寂寂静静
显得春天的山里空而又空。
月亮出来了
惊醒了山里的鸟雀,
听它们
时时地鸣叫在山涧当中。

THE DALE OF SINGING BIRDS

Wang Wei

Sweet laurel blooms fall unenjoyed;

Vague hills dissolve into night void.

The moonrise startles birds to sing;

Their twitters fill the dale with spring.

杂　诗

王　维

其　二

　　君自故乡来，
　　应知故乡事。
　　来日绮窗前，
　　寒梅著花未？

今译

你呀——
是从故乡来，
按理说
应该知道故乡的事。
来那天
在雕绘花纹的窗户前，
也不知
那树寒梅开花没？

OUR NATIVE PLACE

Wang Wei

You come from native place;

What's happened there you'd know.

Did mume blossoms in face

Of my gauze window blow?

相 思

王 维

红豆生南国，
春来发几枝。
愿君多采撷，
此物最相思。

今译

那生长在南国的红豆林，
在这春天来时，也不知发出了几多新枝？
呵，但愿你能多多地采摘，
因为，这东西最能够引人相思。

LOVE SEEDS

Wang Wei

The red beans grow in southern land.

How many load the spring trees!

Gather them till full is your hand!

They would revive fond memories.

静 夜 思

李 白

床前明月光，
疑是地上霜。
举头望明月，
低头思故乡。

今译

床前洒满了月光，
使人怀疑是地上落了一片秋霜。
举起头，我望着明月，
低下头，我思念起自己的故乡。

THOUGHTS ON A STILL NIGHT

Li Bai

Before my bed a pool of light —

Can it be hoarfrost on the ground?

Looking up, I find the moon bright;

Bowing, in homesickness I'm drowned.

秋 浦 歌

李 白

其十五

白发三千丈，
缘愁似个长。
不知明镜里，
何处得秋霜。

头上的白发该有三千丈，
是因为我的愁思像它这样长。
对着镜子，不知在镜子里，
哪儿来这么多的秋霜。

MY WHITE HAIR

Li Bai

Long, long is my whitening hair!

Long, long is it laden with care!

I look into my mirror bright.

From where comes autumn frost in sight?

独坐敬亭山

李 白

众鸟高飞尽,
孤云独去闲。
相看两不厌,
只有敬亭山。

今译

众多的鸟儿
都已经高飞净尽,
一片孤云
自个儿飘走,是那么悠闲。
你看着我
我看着你
谁看谁也不觉得厌倦,
只有我和你呀——敬亭山。

SITTING ALONE IN FACE OF MOUNT JINGTING

Li Bai

All birds have flown away, so high;

A lonely cloud drifts on, so free.

Gazing on Mount Jingting, nor I

Am tired of him, nor he of me.

逢雪宿芙蓉山主人

刘长卿

日暮苍山远，
天寒白屋贫。
柴门闻犬吠，
风雪夜归人。

今译

天晚了
那苍苍茫茫的芙蓉山
看去好像更加遥远，
天冷啊
那茅草小屋显得十分贫寒。
在柴门里
听见几声狗咬，
这时我知道
在风雪中正有夜归的主人。

SEEKING SHELTER IN LOTUS HILL ON A SNOWY NIGHT

Liu Changqing

At sunset hillside village still seems far;

Barren and cold the thatched cottages are.

At wicket gate a dog is heard to bark;

In wind and snow I come when night is dark.

问刘十九

白居易

绿蚁新醅酒，
红泥小火炉。
晚来天欲雪，
能饮一杯无？

今译

我新醅了
一罐绿蚁美酒，
暖酒用的是——
红泥的小火炉。
傍晚以来
眼看着天要下雪，
也不知道你
能不能，同我饮上一杯？

AN INVITATION

Bai Juyi

My new brew gives green glow;

My red clay stove flames up.

At dusk it threatens snow.

Won't you come for a cup?

悯 农

李 绅

其 一

春种一粒粟，
秋成万颗子。
四海无闲田，
农夫犹饿死！

今译

春天
播下一粒粟子，
秋天
就能收下万颗粟子。
四海
没有一处闲置的田地，
农夫呵
还是要被饿死！

THE PEASANTS

Li Shen

I

Each seed peasants sow in spring

Will make autumn yields high.

What will fertile fields bring?

Peasants of hunger die.

悯 农

李 绅

其 二

锄禾日当午,
汗滴禾下土。
谁知盘中餐,
粒粒皆辛苦。

今译

锄地
在日头当午,
汗呵
滴进禾苗下边的泥土。
可谁知道
那碗里的米饭,
一粒一粒
都包含着辛苦!

THE PEASANTS

Li Shen

II

At noon they weed with hoes;

Their sweat drips on the soil.

Each bowl of rice, who knows!

Is the fruit of hard toil.

江 雪

柳宗元

千山鸟飞绝,
万径人踪灭。
孤舟蓑笠翁,
独钓寒江雪。

今译

远处群山中
见不到飞鸟的影子,
近处小路上
看不到行人的踪迹。
这时候
只有一个老渔翁,
驾着小船
披着蓑衣戴着笠
独自,垂钓在寒江的风雪里。

SNOW ON THE RIVER

Liu Zongyuan

From hill to hill no bird in flight;

From path to path no man in sight.

A loncly fisherman afloat

Is fishing snow in lonely boat.

寻隐者不遇

贾 岛

松下问童子,
言师采药去。
只在此山中,
云深不知处。

今译

在那棵老松树底下
我问一个小道童,
他说:
"老师父采药去啦,
只知道
就在这座大山之中,
可是白云重重
也不知道他在哪一处。"

FOR AN ABSENT RECLUSE

Jia Dao

I ask your lad 'neath a pine tree.

"My master's gone for herbs," says he.

"He hides amid the mountains proud

I know not where deep in the cloud."

乐游原

李商隐

向晚意不适，
驱车登古原。
夕阳无限好，
只是近黄昏。

今译

傍晚
心里有些不大舒适，
所以
驾着车子
登上那乐游古原。
呵
夕阳满眼
是一片多好的景色呀，
只可惜
这时候
天已经临近黄昏！

ON THE PLAIN OF TOMBS

Li Shangyin

At dusk my heart is filled with gloom;

I drive my cab to ancient tomb.

The setting sun appears sublime,

O but 'tis near its dying time!

江上渔者

范仲淹

江上往来人,
但爱鲈鱼美。
君看一孤舟,
出没风波里。

在大江上来来往往的人,
都喜爱鲈鱼的鲜美滋味;
可是
请你们看一看
那一片落叶似的小渔船,
它正——
出没在惊涛骇浪中间!

THE FISHERMAN ON THE RIVER

Fan Zhongyan

Those go up and down stream,

Who love delicious bream.

Lo!the fishing boat braves

Perilous winds and waves.

陶 者

梅尧臣

陶尽门前土,
屋上无片瓦。
十指不沾泥,
鳞鳞居大厦。

今译

陶尽了那门前的土,
但自家的屋顶上
却不曾覆盖一片瓦。
两只手儿沾染不到一点儿泥的人,
住着的
却是铺着鳞鳞密瓦的高屋大厦。

THE TILE-MAKER

Mei Yaochen

The clay before his door is dug away

To make his tiles but not to pave his roof.

The rich men's fingers are not soiled with clay;

'Neath scale-like tiles their mansions are cold-proof.

晚过水北

欧阳修

寒川消积雪，
冻浦渐通流。
日暮人归尽，
沙禽上钓舟。

今译

寒冷的川里
初春的积雪已经消融，
冰封的河水
也开始在流动。
天晚了
野外的人已走尽，
沙洲上的鸟儿
都跳上了渔船。

PASSING BY THE NORTHERN SHORE AT DUSK

Ouyang Xiu

On river cold melts heavy snow;

The frozen stream begins to flow.

At sunset all fishermen land;

For fishing boats birds leave the sand.

江　上

王安石

江水漾西风，
江花脱晚红。
离情被横笛，
吹过乱山东。

今 译

江里的水
在荡漾着西风，
江边上的花
已脱尽了晚红。
一阵横笛
勾起了我无限离乡之思，
离乡之思啊
竟被风吹过了乱山之东。

ON THE RIVER

Wang Anshi

The western breeze ripples the streams;

Late flowers shed petals red still.

A flute blows parting grief, it seems,

Beyond the rugged eastern hill.

乌 江

李清照

生当作人杰，
死亦为鬼雄。
至今思项羽，
不肯过江东。

今译

活在世上
应该作人中的豪杰，
即便死了
也要死得壮烈
成为鬼中的英雄。
直到今天
我还在怀念——西楚霸王项羽，
他宁肯在乌江自刎
也不肯——再回江东！

THE BLACK RIVER

Li Qingzhao

Be man of men while you're alive;

Be soul of souls e'en if you're dead!

Think of Xiang Yu who'd not survive

His men whose blood for him was shed!

咏 雪

傅 察

其 一

都城十日雪,
庭户皓已盈。
呼儿试轻扫,
留伴小窗明。

今译

都城
下了十天大雪,
院落里
皓白得已满满盈盈。
喊叫童仆
试着轻轻打扫,
留着一些
伴着我的小窗通明。

SNOW

Fu Cha

I

Here it has snowed from day to day;

My courtyard is all over white.

My son, do not sweep snow away!

For it will keep my window bright.

灯 花

王 质

造化管不得，
要开时便开。
洗天风雨夜，
春色满银台。

今译

大自然
管它不得，
它要开的时候
它就开。
在洗刷苍天大地的
风雨的夜晚，
它开了
就像一天春色
映满了那银色的烛台。

BLOOMING FLAME

Wang Zhi

The flame won't heed the god on high;

It blooms like flowers but won't die.

The rain may wash the sky at night;

Spring's still in view in candlelight.

客 晓

沈受宏

千里作远客，
五更思故乡。
寒鸦数声起，
窗外月如霜。

今译

千里之外
我是离家很远之人，
五更天
竟思念起自己的故乡。
秋天的老鸦
这时几声惊叫振翅飞起，
窗外的月色
就像下了一层白霜。

AT DAWN

Shen Shouhong

I've left my home a thousand miles away;

At early dawn in homesickness I'm lost.

Cold, a few crows' cries wake the break of day;

Out of the window moonlight looks like frost.

舟中夜书所见

查慎行

月黑见渔灯，
孤光一点萤。
微微风簇浪，
散作满河星。

今译

月亮黑黑的
我望见了那远处的渔灯，
孤寂的渔灯
那光就像荧火，一点一点在飘动。
微微的风
拥簇着一层一层的波浪，
又散开去
竟变成了满河星星。

A NIGHT SCENE VIEWED FROM A BOAT

Zha Shenxing

In moonless night a fishing lantern sheds

Like a lonely firefly a feeble gleam.

The light wind raises wave on wave and spreads

A skyful of stars all over the stream.

苔

袁 枚

白日不到处，
青春恰自来。
苔花如米小，
也学牡丹开。

太阳照不到的地方，
春天恰恰自己走来。
青苔的花朵如米粒一样大小，
可是也学那牡丹，一样地开。

MOSS

Yuan Mei

Where sunlight cannot penetrate,

There verdant spring at will may go.

The grain-like moss will imitate

The peony's large flower and grow.

咏 柳

贺知章

碧玉妆成一树高,
万条垂下绿丝绦。
不知细叶谁裁出,
二月春风似剪刀。

今译

那一棵棵柳树
就像翠绿的碧玉妆成
高呵又高,
低垂着的柳条儿
有千缕万缕
恰以绿色的丝绦。
那些细细的小叶儿
也不知是谁给剪出?
二月里,阵阵的春风啊
恰好似一把锋利的剪刀!

THE WILLOW

He Zhizhang

The slender tree is dressed in emerald all about;
Ten thousand branches droop like fringes made of jade.
But do you know by whom these slim leaves are cut out?
The wind of early spring is sharp as scissor blade.

回乡偶书

贺知章

其 一

少小离家老大回,
乡音无改鬓毛衰。
儿童相见不相识,
笑问客从何处来。

今 译

少小的时候离开家
老了以后才回,
一口乡音虽还没改
可是,两鬓的毛发却已衰颓。
孩子们看见了
都不认识,
他们笑着问:
"老头,你从什么地方来?"

HOME COMING

He Zhizhang

I

Young, I left home and not till old do I come back;

My accent is unchanged, my hair no longer black.

The children whom I meet on the way don't know me.

"Where are you from, dear sir?" they smile and ask with glee.

出 塞

王昌龄

其 一

秦时明月汉时关,
万里长征人未还。
但使龙城飞将在,
不教胡马度阴山。

今译

明月还是秦汉时的明月
照临着的边关
还是秦汉时的边关,
长征万里
戍守在边塞的将士们
直到而今
也还是没有返回家园。
我想
只要有使匈奴人丧胆落魄的
那位"飞将军"——李广在,
绝不会像今天这样
让那些胡人的骑兵
经常南侵,跨过阴山。

ON THE FRONTIER

Wang Changling

I

The moon still shines on mountain passes as of yore.

How many guardsmen of the Great Wall are no more!

If the Flying General were still there in command,

No Tartar horses would dare to invade our land.

芙蓉楼送辛渐

王昌龄

寒雨连江夜入吴，
平明送客楚山孤。
洛阳亲友如相问，
一片冰心在玉壶。

今译

在秋雨满江的夜晚
你来到了古代的东吴，
天刚亮
我便在芙蓉楼为你送别
远远望去
那一片楚山呵，使人感到十分孤独。
呵，辛渐
洛阳的那些亲友们
如果问起我的景况，
你就说：
我这颗心哪
仍像一块纯洁的冰一样
——盛在玉壶！

FAREWELL TO XIN JIAN AT LOTUS TOWER

Wang Changling

A cold rain mingled with the Eastern Stream at night;
At dawn you leave the Southern hills lonely in haze.
If my friends in the North should ask if I'm all right,
My heart is free of stain as ice in crystal vase.

九月九日忆山东兄弟

王 维

独在异乡为异客,
每逢佳节倍思亲。
遥知兄弟登高处,
遍插茱萸少一人。

今 译

独自飘泊在外
作他乡之客,
每逢佳节
是格外的思亲。
今天哪
在那遥远的地方
料想兄弟们在那登高之处,
一定都插戴着茱萸呢
可是,却少了我一个人!

THINKING OF MY BROTHERS ON MOUNTAIN-CLIMBING DAY

Wang Wei

Alone, a lonely stranger in a foreign land,

I doubly pine for kinsfolk on a holiday.

I know my brothers would, with dogwood spray in hand,

Climb up the mountain and miss me so far away.

送元二使安西

王 维

渭城朝雨浥轻尘，
客舍青青柳色新。
劝君更尽一杯酒，
西出阳关无故人。

今译

渭城早晨的细雨
润湿了那满地的轻尘，
驿馆里的杨柳
绿蒙蒙一片
颜色显得那般清新。
劝你喝尽这杯酒吧，朋友！
要知道
从这往西
等你出了阳关
便再没有一个故人！

A FAREWELL SONG

Wang Wei

No dust is raised on pathways wet with morning rain;

The willows by the tavern look so fresh and green.

I would ask you to drink a cup of wine again;

West of the Sunny Pass no more friends will be seen.

送沈子福归江东

王 维

杨柳渡头行客稀,
罟师荡桨向临圻。
惟有相思似春色,
江南江北送君归。

今译

在那满是垂柳的渡口
行客啊,很稀很稀,
船夫摇荡着双桨
正去向那远在江东的临圻。
这时候
惟有一片相思
好像这无边的春色,
从江南到江北
满怀着情意送你东归!

SEEING A FRIEND OFF TO THE EAST

Wang Wei

At willow-shaded Ferry passengers are few;

Eastwards into the stream the boatman puts his oars.

Only my longing heart looks like the vernal hue;

It would accompany you along river shores.

黄鹤楼送孟浩然之广陵

李 白

故人西辞黄鹤楼,
烟花三月下扬州。
孤帆远影碧空尽,
惟见长江天际流。

今译

你要走了
朋友
我给你送行
——在这高耸云霄的黄鹤楼头,
是烟花三月天啊
你就要顺流而下
到那淮左名都——扬州。
呵
望着你坐的那只小船的帆影
一点一点地远了
直到碧空的尽处,
这时
能看到的
只有那浩荡的长江
——还在天边上奔流!

SEEING MENG HAORAN OFF AT YELLOW CRANE TOWER

Li Bai

My friend has left the west where the Yellow Crane towers,

For River Town veiled in green willows and red flowers.

His lessening sail is lost in boundless blue sky,

Where I see but the endless River rolling by.

望天门山

李 白

天门中断楚江开，
碧水东流至此回。
两岸青山相对出，
孤帆一片日边来。

今译

浩浩荡荡的楚江
把天门山给冲开，
碧水东流
在这里竟然打旋。
两岸的青山
相对着从江岸上突出，
一叶孤独的小船
飘飘摇摇，从日边而来。

MOUNT HEAVEN'S GATE VIEWED FROM AFAR

Li Bai

Breaking Mount Heaven's Gate, the great River rolls through;
Green billows eastward flow and here turn to the north.
From both sides of the River thrust out the cliffs blue;
Leaving the sun behind, a lonely sail comes forth.

赠 汪 伦

李 白

李白乘舟将欲行，
忽闻岸上踏歌声。
桃花潭水深千尺，
不及汪伦送我情。

今译

李白坐着船将要远行，
忽听到岸边上有踏歌之声。
呵
这桃花潭的水呀深有千尺，
也不如你汪伦——
为我送别的那份深意真情。

TO WANG LUN

Li Bai

I, Li Bai, sit aboard a ship about to go

When suddenly on shore your farewell songs o'erflow.

However deep the Lake of Peach Blossoms may be,

It's not so deep, O Wang Lun, as your love for me.

早发白帝城

李 白

朝辞白帝彩云间，
千里江陵一日还。
两岸猿声啼不住，
轻舟已过万重山。

今译

早晨离开了
那高踞彩云之间的白帝城，
千里远的江陵水程呵
一天就回去啦。
听吧
两岸山里的猿声
不住地在啼唤，
就在这啼唤声里
轻快如飞的小船
已穿过了那万重青山！

LEAVING WHITE EMPEROR TOWN AT DAWN

Li Bai

Leaving at dawn the White Emperor crowned with cloud,

I've sailed a thousand *li* through canyons in a day.

With monkeys' sad adieus the riverbanks are loud;

My skiff has left ten thousand mountains far away.

别 董 大

高 适

千里黄云白日曛，
北风吹雁雪纷纷。
莫愁前路无知己，
天下谁人不识君。

今译

密布千里的黄云
把太阳遮蔽得昏昏沉沉，
一天大雪
纷纷扬扬
呜呜的北风啊
正在吹送南飞的雁群。
但，——走吧董大
你且不要担忧
在前边的路上有没有同心知己，
试问
这普天之下
哪个不认识你——董庭兰君！

FAREWELL TO A LUTIST

Gao Shi

Yellow clouds spread for mile and mile have veiled the day;
The north wind blows down snow and wild geese fly away.
Fear not you've no admirers as you go along!
There is no connoisseur on earth but loves your song.

绝句四首

杜 甫

其 三

两个黄鹂鸣翠柳，
一行白鹭上青天。
窗含西岭千秋雪，
门泊东吴万里船。

今译

草堂前
有两个黄鹂儿
正啼唤在翠绿的杨柳树间，
远处江上
有一行白鹭
飘飘摇摇地
正飞向那一片晴朗的蓝天。
呵
茅屋的窗口
终年可以看到的
是千年不化的西岭岷山的白雪，
柴荆门外
停泊着的
是从东吴来的万里航船！

A QUATRAIN

Du Fu

Two golden orioles sing amid the willows green;

A row of white egrets flies into the blue sky.

My window frames the snow-crowned western mountain scene;

My door oft says to eastward-going ships "Goodbye!"

枫桥夜泊

张　继

月落乌啼霜满天，
江枫渔火对愁眠。
姑苏城外寒山寺，
夜半钟声到客船。

今译

月亮呵下去了
乌鸦仍在啼唤
霜呵，就像把天都给罩满
江边的枫树一丛一丛
渔船里的灯火一闪一闪
它们哪
都在默对着这愁人的睡眠。
听吧
在姑苏城外的那寒山寺里，
半夜间
钟声响起来啦，
那钟声呵
随着秋风
悠悠荡荡地
吹到了我这只载客的小船。

MOORING BY MAPLE BRIDGE AT NIGHT

Zhang Ji

At moonset cry the crows, streaking the frosty sky;

Dimly lit fishing boats 'neath maples sadly lie.

Beyond the city walls, from Temple of Cold Hill,

Bells break the ship-borne roamer's dream and midnight still.

夜 月

刘方平

更深月色半人家,
北斗阑干南斗斜。
今夜偏知春气暖,
虫声新透绿窗纱。

今译

夜深了
月亮也西沉了
这时候,只照着半个人家,
南斗星歪了
北斗星,也已偏斜。
呵
今个晚上
不由得使人感到
那春气已渐渐转暖,
虫声呵
就好像是刚刚——
透进这绿色的窗纱。

A MOONLIT NIGHT

Liu Fangping

The moon has brightened half the house at dead of night;
The slanting Plough and Southern stars shed dying light.
Feeling the warmth of air exhaled by coming spring,
Through my green window screen insects are heard to sing.

滁州西涧

韦应物

独怜幽草涧边生，
上有黄鹂深树鸣。
春潮带雨晚来急，
野渡无人舟自横。

今译

最怜爱那些野草
在西涧边上自生自长，
树丛深处
还有黄莺鸟儿
在那里婉转啼鸣。
潮水呵
夹带着春雨
傍晚显得更急，
野外
因为无人横渡
船哪，被风吹的正在那里打横。

ON THE WEST STREAM AT CHUZHOU

Wei Yingwu

Alone I like the riverside where green grass grows,

And golden orioles sing amid the leafy trees.

With spring showers at dusk the river overflows,

A lonely boat athwart the ferry floats at ease.

早春呈水部张十八员外

韩　愈

其　一

　　天街小雨润如酥，
　　草色遥看近却无。
　　最是一年春好处，
　　绝胜烟柳满皇都。

今译

在皇城的街道上
落的小雨湿润而又细密，
远远望去
那些春草的颜色绿茸茸的
近看又若有若无。
最令人喜爱的景色是这个时候的春天，
可以说
它远远超过了暮春时候烟笼雾罩着柳色
绿满了京都。

EARLY SPRING WRITTEN FOR SECRETARY ZHANG JI

Han Yu

I

The royal streets are moistened by a creamlike rain;

Green grass can be perceived afar but not nearby.

It's the best time of a year late spring tries in vain

With its capital veiled in willows to outvie.

竹 枝 词

刘禹锡

其 一

杨柳青青江水平，
闻郎江上唱歌声。
东边日出西边雨，
道是无晴却有晴。

今译

垂杨柳树青而又青
江水呀，漫平漫平，
这时候，我听到郎哥哥他
正在江上唱歌之声。
呵
东边日头出来
西边又在落着雨
你说是无晴罢
却又有晴。

BAMBOO BRANCH SONG

Liu Yuxi

Between the willows green the river flows along;

My dear one in a boat is heard to sing a song.

The west is veiled in rain;the east enjoys sunshine.

My dear one is as deep in love as day is fine.

望 洞 庭

刘禹锡

湖光秋月两相和,
潭面无风镜未磨。
遥望洞庭山水翠,
白银盘里一青螺。

今译

湖光和秋月
互相照映衬托着
十分和谐,
在洞庭湖面上
一点风都没有
就好像镜子未经过琢磨。
遥望洞庭湖
看那山水一片青翠,
又像在白银盘里放着一个小小的青螺。

LAKE DONGTING VIEWED FROM AFAR

Liu Yuxi

The autumn moon dissolves in soft light of the lake.

Unruffled surface like unpolished mirror bright.

Afar, the isle 'mid water clear without a break

Looks like a spiral shell in a plate silver-white.

暮 江 吟

白居易

一道残阳铺水中,
半江瑟瑟半江红。
可怜九月初三夜,
露似真珠月似弓。

今译

一道残阳
铺在那片水中,
半江变得翠绿翠绿
半江变得通红通红。
最令人怜爱的
是九月初三的夜晚,
露水晶莹得就像珍珠
那弯弯的月亮,就好似一张弓。

SUNSET AND MOONRISE ON THE RIVER

Bai Juyi

The departing sunbeams pave a way on the river;

Half of its waves turn red and the other half shiver.

How I love the third night of the ninth moon aglow!

The dewdrops look like pearls, the crescent like a bow.

秋 夕

杜 牧

银烛秋光冷画屏，
轻罗小扇扑流萤。
天阶夜色凉如水，
坐看牵牛织女星。

今译

银白色的烛光
冷冷清清
照映着
寝宫的画屏，
闲来无事
拿着轻罗小扇
扑捉流萤。
宫殿的石阶上
那一天夜色
冰凉冰凉，就像倾洒下来的一泓秋水，
这时候
我仍呆痴地仰望着那天上的——
牛郎和织女星！

AN AUTUMN NIGHT

Du Mu

Autumn has chilled the painted screen in candlelight;
A silken fan is used to catch flitting fireflies.
The steps seem steeped in water when cold grows the night;
She sits to watch two stars in love meet in the skies.

山　行

杜　牧

远上寒山石径斜，
白云生处有人家。
停车坐爱枫林晚，
霜叶红于二月花。

今译

远远走上秋山
那石头小径
歪歪斜斜，
白云缭绕的地方
还住有几户人家。
停下车来
是因为贪恋枫林的晚景，
你看
那些经霜的叶子
都红过了二月的花！

GOING UPHILL

Du Mu

I go by slanting stony path to the cold hill;

Where rise white clouds, there a sequestered cottage towers.

I stop my cab in maple woods to gaze my fill;

Frost-bitten leaves look redder than early spring flowers.

清 明

杜 牧

清明时节雨纷纷,
路上行人欲断魂。
借问酒家何处有,
牧童遥指杏花村。

今译

清明时节
乍阴乍晴
忽然间又是细雨纷纷,
行走在路上的人哪
面对着这种情景
愁苦得都像要落魄失魂。
遇着人问一声:
"沽酒的店家
在什么地方才有?"
小小的牧童用手指点着——
那远远的杏花村!

THE MOURNING DAY

Du Mu

A drizzling rain falls like tears on the mourning day;

The mourner's heart is going to break on his way.

Where can a wine-shop be found to drown his sad hours?

A cowherd points to a cot 'mid apricot flowers.

夜雨寄北

李商隐

君问归期未有期,
巴山夜雨涨秋池。
何当共剪西窗烛,
却话巴山夜雨时。

今译

你问我归去的日期
我还未定,
今夜
一个人在这巴山驿馆的楼头看雨
雨呀
都涨满了秋天的水池。
怀念你,亲爱的,
可是
要到哪一天
我们才能够相依偎在西窗下
一起剪烛花儿?
那时候
我当低声地对你说:
在巴山看雨的这夜晚
我是怎么样的在思念着你!

WRITTEN ON A RAINY NIGHT TO A FRIEND IN THE NORTH

Li Shangyin

You ask me when I shall return,but I don't know.

It rains in the Western Hills and autumn pools o'erflow.

When shall we trim by windowside the candlelight

And talk about the Western Hills in rainy night?

登飞来峰

王安石

飞来山上千寻塔，
闻说鸡鸣见日升。
不畏浮云遮望眼，
自缘身在最高层。

今译

飞来峰上
有一座千寻高的巍峨古塔，
据说
鸡鸣时刻
攀登上去
能看见旭日东升。
并不怕天上的浮云
能遮住这远望的双眼，
只因为
我的身子
是站在那塔的最高一层！

ON THE WINGED PEAK

Wang Anshi

On the Winged Peak a sky-scraping pagoda towers.
Cocks' crows are heard to wake sunrise at early hours.
Fear not the floating clouds may veil the sun from sight!
For you have placed yourself at the top of the height.

泊船瓜洲

王安石

京口瓜洲一水间，
钟山只隔数重山。
春风又绿江南岸，
明月何时照我还？

今译

那京口和这瓜洲
仅仅相距在一水之间，
远望那钟山
也不过遥隔着数重青山。
呵
温柔的春风
又吹绿了那大江南岸，
可是
天上的明月呀
请问你
要到什么时候
才能够照着我来把家还？

MOORED AT THE FERRY

Wang Anshi

A river severs Northern shore and Southern land;

Between my home and me but a few mountains stand.

The vernal wind has greened the Southern shore again.

When will the moon shine bright on my return? O when?

北陂杏花

王安石

一陂春水绕花身,
花影妖娆各占春。
纵被春风吹作雪,
绝胜南陌碾成尘。

今译

北面池塘的一泓春水
围绕着那些杏花,
娇艳的花和影子
各领风骚,点缀着美好的初春。
可我想
纵然被春风吹落
就像纷纷扬扬的大雪,
也绝对胜过被吹落在田间小路上
被碾踏成尘。

POOLSIDE APRICOT FLOWERS

Wang Anshi

The northern pool surrounds blooming apricot trees,

Their flowers and shadows bewitch the vernal day.

Although blown off like snowflakes by the vernal breeze,

They shame the petals ground to dust on southern way.

春日偶成

程 颢

云淡风轻近午天，
傍花随柳过前川。
时人不识余心乐，
将谓偷闲学少年。

今译

云儿淡淡
风儿轻轻
这已是近午的时候，
在野花翠柳中穿行
来到了前面的小河边。
世俗的人们
并不了解我心里有什么快乐，
他们可能认为
我不过是忙里偷闲
在学那些轻浮少年！

IMPROMPTU LINES ON A SPRING DAY

Cheng Hao

Towards noon fleecy clouds waft in the gentle breeze;
I cross the stream amid flowers and willow trees.
What do the worldlings know about my inward pleasure?
They would but take me for a truant fond of leisure.

六月二十七日望湖楼醉书

苏 轼

其 一

黑云翻墨未遮山，
白雨跳珠乱入船。
卷地风来忽吹散，
望湖楼下水如天。

今译

乌黑的云彩
就像墨被打翻
但是，还没有——遮满那山，
白色的雨点儿
像散乱的珍珠
噼噼叭叭地，跳进了小船。
一阵直卷地面的大风
吹过来
忽然把云彩给吹散，
这时候
那望湖楼下的水呀
——就像是碧蓝碧蓝的天！

WRITTEN WHILE DRUNKEN IN LAKE VIEW PAVILION

Su Shi

I

Dark clouds like spilt ink spread over the mountains quiet;
Raindrops like bouncing pearls into the boat run riot.
A sudden rolling gale dispels clouds far and nigh;
Calmed water in the lake becomes one with the sky.

饮湖上初晴后雨

苏 轼

其 二

水光潋滟晴方好，
山色空濛雨亦奇。
欲把西湖比西子，
淡妆浓抹总相宜。

水光闪动着
天晴的时候，方显得美好，
山色迷濛
落雨的时候，看上去也十分新奇。
呵
如果要把西湖——
比成西施那样的美女，
真是
不论淡妆，还是浓抹
总都——非常相宜。

DRINKING AT THE LAKE FIRST IN SUNNY, THEN IN RAINY, WEATHER

Su Shi

II

The brimming waves delight the eyes on sunny days,

The dimming hills present rare view in rainy haze.

West Lake may be compared to Lady of the West,

Whether she is richly adorned or plainly dressed.

题西林壁

苏 轼

横看成岭侧成峰,
远近高低各不同。
不识庐山真面目,
只缘身在此山中。

今译

横着看成了山岭
侧着看便成了山峰,
远
近
高
低
都各不相同。
人们
认识不清
庐山的真实面目,
只是因为——
身在此山之中!

WRITTEN ON THE WALL OF WEST FOREST TEMPLE

Su Shi

It's a range viewed in face and peaks viewed from one side,

Assuming different shapes viewed from far and wide.

Of Mount Lu we cannot make out the true face,

For we are lost in the heart of the very place.

惠崇春江晓景

苏　轼

竹外桃花三两枝，
春江水暖鸭先知。
蒌蒿满地芦芽短，
正是河豚欲上时。

今译

翠竹外面
正开着桃花三枝两枝，
春天来了
江水也暖了
鸭子们最先得知。
呵
你们看
蒌蒿长了满地
那芦芽儿
还很短很短，
这时候
应该正是河豚——
快要上市之时！

VERNAL SCENE ON A RIVER

Su Shi

Beyond bamboos a few twigs of peach blossoms blow;

When spring has warmed the stream, ducks are the first to know.

By waterside short reeds bud and wild flowers teem;

It is just time for the globefish to swim upstream.

初见嵩山

张 耒

年来鞍马困尘埃,
赖有青山豁我怀。
日暮北风吹雨去,
数峰清瘦出云来。

今 译

数年来,骑在马上
东奔西走
总被困顿在尘埃之中,
所幸的是
还有青山
能使我豁达心胸。
天晚了
北风吹着一场冷雨而去,
有数座清瘦的山峰
露出了那片云彩来。

AT FIRST SIGHT OF MOUNT SONG

Zhang Lei

Weary for years of toilsome journey on my way,

My mind is happy at the sight of mountains green.

The northern wind at dusk has blown the rain away;

Out of the clouds emerge frowning peaks long and lean.

春 游 湖

徐 俯

双飞燕子几时回，
夹岸桃花蘸水开。
春雨断桥人不渡，
小舟撑出柳阴来。

今译

一对一对的小燕子
也不知几时才飞回？
两岸飞谢的桃花呀
正蘸着水儿流开。
春雨落着
小桥被隔断了
人已经无法渡过，
恰好
正在这时候
有一只小船
从柳阴中
——撑了出来！

A SPRING DAY ON THE LAKE

Xu Fu

When will the swallows pair by pair fly back again?
Peach blossoms on both shores just above water float.
I cannot cross the bridge submerged by vernal rain.
What joy to see from willow shade come out a boat!

病　牛

李　纲

耕犁千亩实千箱，
力尽筋疲谁复伤。
但得众生皆得饱，
不辞羸病卧残阳。

今译

犁地耕田有千亩
装满了很多很多粮仓，
力尽了
又有谁来把我哀怜？
只要使普天之下的众生
都能够得到温饱，
我并不怕
又瘦又病
寂寞地卧对着残阳。

TO A SICK BUFFALO

Li Gang

You've ploughed field on field and reaped crop on crop of grain.
Who would pity you when you are tired out and done?
If old and young could eat their fill, then you would fain
Exhaust yourself and lie sick in the setting sun.

晓出净慈送林子方

杨万里

毕竟西湖六月中，
风光不与四时同。
接天莲叶无穷碧，
映日荷花别样红。

今译

六月
在西湖之上，
论风光景色
到底和四时不同。
你看，
那远接蓝天的一片莲叶
无边无际，碧绿碧绿，
那映着阳光的荷花
一朵一朵，通红通红。

THE LAKESIDE TEMPLE AT DAWN

Yang Wanli

The uncommon West Lake in the midst of sixth moon
Displays a scenery to other months unknown.
Green lotus leaves outspread as far as boundless sky;
Pink lotus blossoms take from sunshine a new dye.

闲居初夏午睡起

杨万里

其 一

梅子留酸软齿牙,
芭蕉分绿与窗纱。
日长睡起无情思,
闲看儿童捉柳花。

今译

望着梅子
仿佛闻到酸味
都酸麻了齿牙,
芭蕉的影子
照映着,把绿色分给了窗纱。
天气渐长
午睡醒了以后,无情无绪,
这时候
闲得无聊
我在看那些儿童们
扑捉柳花!

RISING AFTER A SIESTA IN EARLY SUMMER

Yang Wanli

The aftertaste of mumes has left my teeth still sour;

Banana leaves diffuse their green to window screen.

Indolent after a siesta of long, long hour,

I watch children catch willow-down. What joyful mien!

过松源晨炊漆公店

杨万里

莫言下岭便无难,
赚得行人错喜欢。
正入万山圈子里,
一山放出一山拦。

今译

不要说下山便再没有什么艰难,
只骗得行旅之人错误地暗自喜欢。
不信你看
正进入万山的圈子里,
一山放过行人,一山又在阻挡。

PASSING BY SONGYUAN

Yang Wanli

Don't say downhill no obstacles before you lie,

Misleading wayfarers to be happy and gay!

You are surrounded by ten thousand mountains high:

One mountain lets you pass, another bars your way.

秋夜将晓出篱门迎凉有感

陆　游

其　二

三万里河东入海，
五千仞岳上摩天。
遗民泪尽胡尘里，
南望王师又一年。

今译

三万里的黄河
浩浩荡荡
流向东洋大海，
五千仞的华山
巍巍峨峨
仿佛挨到青天。
可是
被遗弃在金人统治下的人民
眼泪都已淌干，
天天南望着王师北伐
却眼巴巴地
过了一年又一年！

EARLY DAWN AT MY WICKET GATE

Lu You

The long,long River flows eastward into the sea;

The high,high Mountains looking upward scrape the sky.

The refugees have shed all their tears in debris;

Another year will pass,no royal army's nigh.

十一月四日风雨大作

陆　游

僵卧孤村不自哀，
尚思为国戍轮台。
夜阑卧听风吹雨，
铁马冰河入梦来。

今译

虽然是困居在孤寂的山村里
但并不觉得有什么悲哀，
为了报效国家
还想望着
去防守那边城轮台！
呵
当三更半夜间
躺在床上
默听着呼啸的狂风吹着暴雨，
这一晚上
披着铁甲的战马呀
千里冰封的北地的河流呵
都一齐涌到——
我的梦里！

THE STORM ON THE FOURTH DAY OF THE ELEVENTH MOON

Lu You

Forlorn in a cold bed, I'm grieved not for my plight,
Still thinking of recovering our lost frontiers.
Hearing the stormy wind blow rain at dead of night,
I dreamed of frozen River crossed by cavaliers.

梅花绝句

陆　游

闻道梅花坼晓风，
雪堆遍满四山中。
何方可化身千亿，
一树梅前一放翁。

今 译

听说
那梅花在晓风中已绽开，
像雪一样堆遍了
那四面的山中。
有什么办法
我的身子能够化作千亿万亿，
一树梅花跟前
都让它有一个陆放翁！

A QUATRAIN ON MUME BLOSSOMS

Lu You

'Tis said against cold morning wind mume blossoms blow

All over four mountains like pile on pile of snow.

Could I be multiplied into ten thousand me,

You would find my person before every mume tree.

示 儿

陆 游

死去元知万事空，
但悲不见九州同。
王师北定中原日，
家祭无忘告乃翁。

今译

原也知道
死去以后一切的事情都成空，
还是悲伤
看不到这九州的河山重归一统。
呵
当朝廷的军队北伐
平定了中原之日，
在你们举行家祭的时候
不要忘记了把这喜信
告诉你们的父亲！

TESTAMENT TO MY SONS

Lu You

I know that after death everything will be vain,

But I'm grieved not to see our country reunite.

When Royal Armies recover the Central Plain,

Do not forget to tell your sire in sacred rite!

四时田园杂兴

范成大

其四十四

新筑场泥镜面平,
家家打稻趁霜晴。
笑歌声里轻雷动,
一夜连枷响到明。

新筑的场院
那泥土碾得像镜子一般溜平,
家家户户打稻子
都趁着下霜以后的晴天。
在欢声笑语中
轻轻的雷声响动
怕又要下雨呀
一夜间的连枷之声,直响到天明。

RURAL LIFE IN AUTUMN

Fan Chengda

Flat as mirror is the newly-built threshing ground;
From house to house the grain is beaten in sunlight.
In songs and laughters even thunder would be drowned;
The flail is wielded pitter-patter through the night.

横 塘

范成大

南浦春来绿一川,
石桥朱塔两依然。
年年送客横塘路,
细雨垂杨系画船。

今译

当春天来到南浦的时候
满河都绿绿汪汪,
那古老的石桥呵
那朱红的宝塔呀
依旧和从前一般。
而我
年年为朋友们送行
在这横塘路上,
常常都是于细雨濛濛之中
那垂杨柳树上
拴着画船。

THE LAKESIDE LANE

Fan Chengda

Spring has come and greened all over the southern land;

The stone bridge and red tower face to face still stand.

From year to year friends are seen off on Lakeside Lane;

The weeping willow would tie their boat in fine rain.

春 日

朱 熹

胜日寻芳泗水滨，
无边光景一时新。
等闲识得东风面，
万紫千红总是春。

今译

在一个晴朗的日子
我在泗水之滨郊游赏花，
无边无际的
春天的风光，焕然一新。
随时我都能够
感觉到东风那温柔的容貌，
百花盛开
万紫千红
这里那里，都呵是春。

A SPRING DAY

Zhu Xi

I seek for spring by riverside on a fine day.

O what refreshing sight does the boundless view bring!

I find the face of east wind in an easy way;

Myriads of reds and violets only reveal spring.

水口行舟

朱 熹

其 一

昨夜扁舟雨一蓑，
满江风浪夜如何。
今朝试卷孤篷看，
依旧青山绿树多。

今译

昨夜里
在小船上
雨下得好大呀，我都披上了蓑衣，
满江都是风浪
也不知道
造成了什么样的后果？
今天早晨
卷起那船帘子来看，
没想到
依旧是满目青山
绿树还是那样的多！

BOATING AFTER A STORMY NIGHT

Zhu Xi

A straw-cloaked man sailed a leaflike boat last night.
Could it brave winds and waves when storm was at its height?
Opening the awning at dawn, what do I see
But blue hill on blue hill and green tree on green tree!

观书有感

朱 熹

半亩方塘一鉴开,
天光云影共徘徊。
问渠那得清如许,
为有源头活水来。

半亩方方的池塘
就像一面新打磨的镜子,
天光呵
云影呵
一齐在里边流荡徘徊。
问它
怎么会
如此这般地清清澈澈?
原来呀
是因为有活水不断地——
从源头流来!

THE BOOK

Zhu Xi

There lies a glassy oblong pool,

Where light and shade pursue their course.

How can it be so clear and cool?

For water comes fresh from its source.

题临安邸

林 升

山外青山楼外楼，
西湖歌舞几时休。
暖风熏得游人醉，
直把杭州作汴州。

今译

山外还有青山
楼外还有高楼，
请问
这西湖之上的歌舞
要到什么时候才能停止？
温软的东风
熏得那些游人都昏昏欲醉，
你看他们
简直是把这行都杭州
当成了已沦亡的故都汴州！

WRITTEN IN THE NEW CAPITAL

Lin Sheng

Hills rise beyond blue hills,towers beyond high towers.

When will West Lake end its singing and dancing hours?

The revelers are drunk with vernal breeze and leisure;

They'd take the new capital for old place of pleasure.

约　客

赵师秀

黄梅时节家家雨，
青草池塘处处蛙。
有约不来过夜半，
闲敲棋子落灯花。

今译

黄梅时节
整天哪都在下雨，
在青草池塘里
咕咯咕咯
到处都是鸣蛙。
本有约会
但不见人来
这时候
已经过了夜半，
闲得无聊
我敲打着棋子
却震落了灯花！

A PROMISE BROKEN

Zhao Shixiu

In rainy season house on house is steeped in rain;
On poolside meadow here and there frogs croak in vain.
My friend comes not on promise till well past midnight.
What can I do but play chess alone by lamplight!

乡村四月

翁　卷

绿遍山原白满川，
子规声里雨如烟。
乡村四月闲人少，
才了蚕桑又插田。

今译

草木都绿遍了山岗
白茫茫的水呀
也涨满了前面的小河川，
杜鹃正啼唤着呢
就在这啼唤声里
那一天细雨呀
迷迷蒙蒙，如雾如烟。
呵
在乡村的四月里
空闲着的人很少很少，
你们看
刚刚忙完了蚕桑
紧接着又要插秧种田！

THE COUNTRYSIDE IN THE FOURTH MOON

Weng Juan

The hills and plains are green all o'er and streams are white;
Amid the cuckoos' songs rain falls as smoke in sight.
In the fourth moon few peasants from farmwork are freed;
Transplanting rice seedlings, they have silkworms to feed.

寒 夜

杜 耒

寒夜客来茶当酒，
竹炉汤沸火初红。
寻常一样窗前月，
才有梅花便不同。

今译

在寒冷的夜里
客人来了，常常都是拿茶当酒，
小小竹炉里水已烧开
那火却刚刚发红。
与平常一样的窗前明月，
因为
梅花开了，
便使人觉得不同！

A COLD NIGHT

Du Lei

I've no wine in cold night, my friend drinks tea instead;
I boil water on a bamboo stove glowing red.
The moon above my window still sheds the same light,
But with mume blossoms blowing, it shines with delight.

村　晚

雷　震

草满池塘水满陂，
山衔落日浸寒漪。
牧童归去横牛背，
短笛无腔信口吹。

今译

草长满了池塘
水也漫平了池塘的两岸，
山
含着落下去的太阳
泛起一道寒冷的清光。
归去的牧童
横坐在牛背上，
那支短笛也没个腔调
只是信口地乱吹。

A VILLAGE AT DUSK

Lei Zhen

With poolside overgrown with grass,pools overflow,
Hills swallow setting sun and ripples feel the chill.
The herdsboy goes back,astride on a buffalo;
He plays at random on a flute what tune he will.

游园不值

叶绍翁

应怜屐齿印苍苔,
小扣柴扉久不开。
春色满园关不住,
一枝红杏出墙来。

今译

应是怜惜
被木鞋的小齿
踏出痕迹的那些青苔,
轻轻地
敲打着柴门
许久许久
也没人来开。
可是
那满园的春色
总还是关锁不住,
不信你看
有一枝红杏
竟伸到了那大墙外边来!

A CLOSED GARDEN

Ye Shaoweng

The green moss cannot bear the sabots whose teeth sting;

The wicket gate is closed to me who tap and call.

The garden cannot shut up the full blooming spring;

An apricot stretches out a branch o'er the wall.

春暮游小园

王 淇

一从梅粉褪残妆，
涂抹新红上海棠。
开到荼蘼花事了，
丝丝天棘出莓墙。

今译

自从梅花
像美人一样卸了妆，
春天又把那鲜艳的红色
涂上了盛开的海棠。
满架荼蘼开过以后
春天的花也已经开罢，
这时候
只有那伸展着新丝的天门冬
把枝儿探出了长满苔藓的矮墙。

LATE SPRING IN A GARDEN

Wang Qi

Since the pink petals of mume blossoms fade away,

The crabapples paint red their flowers one and all.

After roseleaf raspberries their beauty display,

Threads of asparagus creep o'er the mossy wall.

溪桥晚兴

郑 协

寂寞亭基野渡边,
春流平岸草芊芊。
一川晚照人闲立,
满袖杨花听杜鹃。

今译

破败寂寞的亭基
在山野过渡的渡口边,
春天
水流淌得涨平了河岸
草也是那般茂盛可观。
夕阳西下的余光照着河川
人啊,在那里悠闲地站立,
杨花落了满袖子
我在听那唱着"不如归去"的杜鹃。

ONE EVENING ON A BRIDGE OVER THE BROOK

Zheng Xie

A lonely ruined tower stands by ferry side;

Grass overruns the shore leveled with the spring tide.

At sunset on the stream leisurely I stand long

To hear 'mid willowdown cuckoos' homegoing song.

溪 上

刘 因

坐久苍苔如见侵,
携筇随水就轻阴。
松声似厌滩声小,
云影旋移山色深。

今 译

久久地，坐在苍苔之上
就好像也被青苔给侵染，
拿着拐杖
随着流水
我找一处地方遮住那薄薄的阴凉。
松树的声音
似乎讨厌那溪水的声音太小，
云彩的影子移动着
山的颜色立刻变得很深很深。

ON THE BROOK

Liu Yin

I sit so long 'mid moss as to see green invade;

I follow, cane in hand, the stream to a light shade.

The rippling pine trees overwhelm the rippling brook;

The floating clouds seem to darken the mountain's look.

白　梅

王　冕

冰雪林中着此身，
不与桃李混芳尘。
忽然一夜清香发，
散作乾坤万里春。

今译

我站立在有冰有雪的树林之中，
并不与桃花李花
混在一起，沦落在世俗的尘埃当中。
忽然间
这一夜
清新的香味散发出来，
竟散作了天地间的
万里新春。

THE WHITE MUME BLOSSOMS

Wang Mian

You look so pure in the forest of ice and snow;
With peach and plum blossoms for splendor you won't vie.
Suddenly one night your fragrance begins to flow,
It will spread out and turn into spring far and nigh.

墨 梅

王 冕

我家洗砚池头树，
朵朵花开淡墨痕。
不要人夸颜色好，
只留清气满乾坤。

今译

我家洗砚池前的
那棵墨梅树，
一朵朵花都开了
开得留有淡墨色的娇痕。
不要人夸它们的颜色
是如何娇好，
只要留得那股馨香之气
充满这大好乾坤。

MUME BLOSSOMS PAINTED IN BLACK INK

Wang Mian

Beside our ancestor's inky pool grows a tree;

Each and every flower bears the pale inky trace.

It needs no one to praise its color in high glee,

For it will leave on earth but its uncommon grace.

海乡竹枝词

杨维桢

其 一

潮来潮退白洋沙，
白洋女儿把锄耙。
苦海熬干是何日，
免得侬来爬雪沙。

今 译

潮水来了
潮水又退了
在这白洋沙头，
白洋沙头的儿女们
用锄头把沙地疏耙。
那苦海熬干
也不知要到哪一天，
熬干了呀
也免得我天天来疏耙那盐滩！

A SEASIDE BAMBOO BRANCH SONG

Yang Weizhen

The tides flow in and out and leave salt on the sand;

The seaside maidens rake salt in piles, tool in hand.

When will the bitter sea be dried of its bitter grain;

Lest we should rake snow-white salt in with might and main?

石 灰 吟

于 谦

千锤万击出深山，
烈火焚烧若等闲。
粉骨碎身全不怕，
要留清白在人间。

今译

经过千锤万击
才走出深山，
烈火焚烧着
却视若等闲。
粉身碎骨了
全都不怕，
只要留下这一身清白
在这大好人间。

SONG OF THE LIME

Yu Qian

The lime comes out of mountains after hammer blows;

Through tortures of great flaming fire harmless it goes.

Though broken into pieces, it stands in no fear,

Determined to make a white-washed world clean and clear.

夏口夜泊别友人

李梦阳

黄鹤楼前日欲低，
汉阳城树乱乌啼。
孤舟夜泊东游客，
恨杀长江不向西。

今译

黄鹤楼前的太阳
已经渐渐西垂，
汉阳城里的树上
乌鸦在胡乱地啼飞。
孤独的小船里
泊睡着的是东游之客，
令人恨那长江呵，
只是东流，而不向西。

FAREWELL TO A FRIEND AT YELLOW CRANE TOWER

Li Mengyang

Before Yellow Crane Tower the sun hangs low;

Around the trees by city wall cries crow on crow.

In a lonely boat moored at night, eastward I'd go.

How I regret the River would not westward flow!

竹 枝 词

袁宏道

其 四

侬家生长在河干，
夫婿如鱼不去滩。
冬夜趁霜春趁水，
芦花被底一生寒。

今 译

我家就住在这
大河的河边，
丈夫他就像那鱼儿
总是离不开河滩。
冬天趁着霜
春天趁着水，
在那芦花被的被底
一辈子都是那么清寒。

BAMBOO BRANCH SONG

Yuan Hongdao

My family lives all the year by riverside;

Like fish in water my husband won't leave household.

He braves the winter frost and goes out with spring tide;

In a quilt of reed catkins we feel our life cold.

真州绝句

王士禛

其　四

江干多是钓人居,
柳陌菱塘一带疏。
好是日斜风定后,
半江红树卖鲈鱼。

今　译

江边上
打鱼人多半住在那里,
在那杨柳巷陌和菱花塘边
房屋十分稀疏。
最好的时光
是太阳偏西风平以后,
这时候
半江都是映红的树影
而他们正在叫卖鲈鱼。

A QUATRAIN ON THE NORTHERN SHORE

Wang Shizhen

Many are fishermen's huts on the rivershore,

And lotus ponds girt with a row of willow trees.

At sunset half the river reddens, what is more,

We like the breams sold 'neath maples in gentle breeze.

蒙 阴

厉 鹗

冲风苦爱帽檐斜，
历尾无多感岁华。
却向东蒙看霁雪，
青天乱插玉莲花。

今译

顶着风
我非常喜欢帽子被春风
吹得歪歪斜斜，
看历书已到了年终岁尾
我不禁感慨起已逝的年华。
回过头向着东蒙山看那天晴以后的
积雪的山头，
更好像乱插了好多盛开的白莲花。

MOUNT MENG

Li E

The slanting peak of my cap helps me brave the breeze;
The year will soon expire and I feel ill at ease.
I look eastward to snow-crowned Mount Meng in sunlight;
Studded with jadelike lotus blooms, the sky is bright.

竹 石

郑 燮

咬定青山不放松，
立根原在破岩中。
千磨万击还坚劲，
任尔东西南北风。

今译

狠狠咬住那青山
不肯放松，
原本深深地
扎根在石缝当中。
虽经千磨万击
可身子骨仍很坚韧，
任凭你刮
东西南北风。

BAMBOO IN THE ROCK

Zheng Xie

The firm bamboo bites into the green mountain steep;
Its toothlike root in broken rock is planted deep.
Steady and strong though struck and beaten without rest,
It cares not if the wind blows north, south, east or west.

新 雷

张维屏

造物无言却有情,
每于寒尽觉春生。
千红万紫安排着,
只待新雷第一声。

今译

大自然默默无语
但却很有感情,
每当严寒消尽了
就会感觉到那春天已经来临。
明天
万紫千红都已经安排妥当,
百花先后怒放
只等着春雷一声。

THE FIRST THUNDER

Zhang Weiping

Nature is mute but has a heart,

To feel spring come and winter part.

All flowers are ready to burst,

But wait for thunder to roar first.

己亥杂诗

龚自珍

其 五

浩荡离愁白日斜,
吟鞭东指即天涯。
落红不是无情物,
化作春泥更护花。

今 译

离开都城的时候
那无边无际的离愁弥漫着
这时候,太阳已经西斜
诗人的鞭子指向东方
那里就是万里天涯。
呵
纷纷扬扬的落花
并不是无情之物,
即便粉身碎骨、化作春泥
还是要培育那新开的花。

MISCELLANIES OF THE YEAR 1839

Gong Zizhen

V

My parting grief is boundless when the sun hangs low,
Eastward points my whip and far away I'll go.
The fallen blossoms are not an unfalling thing,
Though turned to mud, they'd quicken flowers' growth next spring.

己亥杂诗

龚自珍

其一百二十五

九州生气恃风雷，
万马齐喑究可哀。
我劝天公重抖擞，
不拘一格降人才。

今译

中国的勃勃生气
仰仗着的是那激荡的风雷，
万马一时都喑哑无声
毕竟使人痛感可哀。
我奉劝老天
重新振作起来，精神抖擞，
不要拘泥于一种模式
降生栋梁之才。

MISCELLANIES OF THE YEAR 1839

Gong Zizhen

CXXV

From wind and thunder comes a nation's vital force.

What a great pity not to hear a neighing horse!

I urge the Lord of Heaven to brace up again,

And send down talents of all kinds to the Central Plain.

狱中题壁

谭嗣同

望门投止思张俭，
忍死须臾待杜根。
我自横刀向天笑，
去留肝胆两昆仑。

今译

在狱中
思念那逃亡的师友
我想到东汉时投住无门的张俭，
忍痛等死
我又怀念起死里逃生的杜根。
我自己
横握着刀不禁仰天大笑，
无论死去还是留在世上
我的那些战友们
都肝胆相照，好似两座耸立着的昆仑。

WRITTEN ON THE WALL OF THE PRISON

Tan Sitong

You may seek refuge to preserve our nation's strength;

I will die soon to awake our people at length.

I brave the sword o'erhead and laugh towards the sky;

Stay or leave, live or die, our minds stand mountain-high.

送杜少府之任蜀州

王 勃

城阙辅三秦,风烟望五津。
与君离别意,同是宦游人。
海内存知己,天涯若比邻。
无为在歧路,儿女共沾巾。

今 译

辅佐帝都长安的——
有雍州、塞州和翟州这三秦,
透过风烟
便可以望到那——
白华、万里、江首、涉头和江南五津。
在与你离别的时候
你我心里都充满了
无限惜别的情意,
因为我们
同样是——
在宦海之中浮沉游荡的人。

我想
只要在这四海之内
能有你这样一个同心知己,
即使远隔在天涯
也应当说是——
近在比邻。
呵
走吧,朋友,
且不要在我们即将分手的
叉路口上,
像那些小儿女们似的
让珠泪洒满佩巾!

FAREWELL TO PREFECT DU

Wang Bo

You'll leave the town walled far and wide

For mist-veiled land by riverside.

I feel on parting sad and drear,

For both of us are strangers here.

If you have friends who know your heart,

Distance cannot keep you apart.

At crossroads where we bid adieu,

Do not shed tears as women do!

望月怀远

张九龄

海上生明月,天涯共此时。
情人怨遥夜,竟夕起相思。
灭烛怜光满,披衣觉露滋。
不堪盈手赠,还寝梦佳期。

今译

大海之上,
升起了一轮明月,
任你在天涯海角
也能共同享有这样美好时刻。
望月的有情之人
怎能不怨尤这漫漫的长夜,
而我呀
整夜都勾起了对你的相思。
熄了蜡烛
爱怜这银白的月光充满整个世界
披上衣服,走到中庭
不觉感到秋露在滋生。
这些月光啊
不可能捧上一把赠送给你,
我只好回到梦中。

LOOKING AT THE MOON AND LONGING FOR ONE FAR AWAY

Zhang Jiuling

Over the sea grows the moon bright;

We gaze on it far, far apart.

Lovers complain of long, long night;

They rise and long for the dear heart.

Candle blown out, fuller is light;

My coat put on, I'm moist with dew.

As I can't hand you moonbeams white,

I go to bed to dream of you.

过故人庄

孟浩然

故人具鸡黍，邀我至田家。
绿树村边合，青山郭外斜。
开轩面场圃，把酒话桑麻。
待到重阳日，还来就菊花。

老朋友备下了
丰富的酒和饭，
邀我来到了
这庄户人家。
四周的绿树
把小村庄环绕，
青青的山峦
立在村郭外边，似乎有些倾斜。
打开窗子

面对的是谷场和园圃，
一起饮酒
共同话题是农事和桑麻。
啊
等到了
重阳节那天，
我还要来呢
同你一起观赏菊花！

VISITING AN OLD FRIEND

Meng Haoran

My friend's prepared chicken and rice

And invit'd me to cottage hall.

Green trees surround the village nice;

Blue hills slant beyond city wall.

Windows open to field and ground;

O'er wine we talk of crop of grain.

On Double Ninth Day I'll come round

For his chrysanthemums again.

次北固山下

王 湾

客路青山外，行舟绿水前。
潮平两岸阔，风正一帆悬。
海日生残夜，江春入旧年。
乡书何处达，归雁洛阳边。

今译

旅客走的路
在青青的北固山外，
一叶小舟，慢慢行进
在碧绿的江水之前。
潮水上涨
那两岸显得更加宽阔，
风很顺畅
一片孤帆，在桅杆上高高悬挂。
海上的红日
在黑夜将残的时候就升起，
大江上的春意
早已透进了将尽的旧年。
啊
一纸乡书
到何时才能到达？
只有拜托北归的鸿雁
捎到洛阳城边！

PASSING BY BEIGU MOUNTAIN

Wang Wan

My boat goes by the green mountain high

And passes through the river blue.

The banks seem wide at the full tide;

A sail with ease hangs in soft breeze.

The sun brings light born of last night;

New spring invades old year which fades.

How can I send word to my friend?

Homing wild geese, fly northward please!

使至塞上

王 维

单车欲问边，属国过居延。
征蓬出汉塞，归雁入胡天。
大漠孤烟直，长河落日圆。
萧关逢候骑，都护在燕然。

今译

轻车简从
要去慰问边防战士，
走过附属国
甘肃西北的居延。
像飘动的蓬草
走出汉家的边塞，
北归的大雁
已进入胡人的蓝天。
在大漠上

那孤独的狼烟点着了，上升得
很直很直，
万里黄河上西沉的太阳
显得很圆很圆。
在萧关
我遇见了侦察的骑兵，
说督护他
正在燕然山——最前线！

ON MISSION TO THE FRONTIER

Wang Wei

A single carriage goes to the frontier;

An envoy crosses northwest mountains high.

Like tumbleweed I leave our fortress drear;

As wild geese I come 'neath Tartarian sky.

In boundless desert lonely smoke rises straight;

Over endless river the sun sinks round.

I meet a cavalier at the camp gate;

In Northern Fort the general will be found.

汉江临眺

王 维

楚塞三湘接，荆门九派通。
江流天地外，山色有无中。
郡邑浮前浦，波澜动远空。
襄阳好风日，留醉与山翁。

今 译

楚国的边塞
漓湘、潇湘、蒸湘这三湘相接，
荆门山下
长江九条支流连通。
大江呵远去
就像奔流在天地之外，
岸边的青山，时隐时现
就仿佛在忽有忽无之中。
前边的城镇
宛如在江水之中上下浮动，
波涛奔涌
那远处的天空，也像是在晃动。
呵
古老的襄阳呵
风物美好，到处是晴空朗日，
我愿意留下来
喝得酩酊大醉，陪伴你——
山简老翁。

A VIEW OF THE HAN RIVER

Wang Wei

Three southern rivers rolling by,

Nine tributaries meeting here,

Their water flows from earth to sky;

Hills now appear,now disappear.

Towns seem to float on rivershore;

With waves horizons rise and fall.

Such scenery as we adore

Would make us drink and drunken all.

终 南 山

王 维

太乙近天都,连山到海隅。
白云回望合,青霭入看无。
分野中峰变,阴晴众壑殊。
欲投人处宿,隔水问樵夫。

今 译

太乙峰高入云霄
临近天都,
连绵的山峦
一直延伸到了大海之滨。
行走在山路上
回头望去,身后白云合成一片,
雾气缭绕,当你进入其中
又觉得一切已无影无踪。

地域之阔
一峰之隔,便属于不同的分野,
同一个时辰
山间的阴晴明暗也各不相同。
呵
我真想找一处人家投宿,
可是没有人烟
只好隔着涧水
去询问那——打柴的樵夫。

MOUNT ETERNAL SOUTH

Wang Wei

The highest peak scrapes the sky blue;

It extends from hills to the sea.

When I look back, clouds shut the view;

When I come near, I see mist flee.

Peaks vary in north and south side;

Vales differ in sunshine or shade.

Seeking a lodging to abide,

I ask a woodcutter for aid.

渡荆门送别

李 白

渡远荆门外,来从楚国游。
山随平野尽,江入大荒流。
月下飞天镜,云生结海楼。
仍怜故乡水,万里送行舟。

今译

告别巴蜀,渡过三峡　　　　　就像天上飞下来的一轮明镜,
来到这荆门山外,　　　　　　云彩升起,光怪陆离。
我呀　　　　　　　　　　　　忽然怜爱起那——
又来到了楚国漫游。　　　　　故乡的水,
山势,随着平坦的旷野无穷无尽,万里迢迢
江水,正在无边的大地上奔流。伴随着这远去的行舟。
月亮映在大江里

BEYOND MOUNT THORN-GATE

Li Bai

Leaving Mount Thorn-Gate far away,

My boat pursues its eastward way.

Mountains end where begins the plain;

The river rolls to boundless main.

The moon's a mirror from the sky;

Clouds look like miraged towers high.

The water which from homeland flows

Will follow me where my boat goes.

秋登宣城谢朓北楼

李　白

江城如画里，山晚望晴空。
两水夹明镜，双桥落彩虹。
人烟寒橘柚，秋色老梧桐。
谁念北楼上，临风怀谢公。

今译

秋天
宣城北楼就像在画图里，
傍晚时，望着陵阳山、敬亭山
是一片晴朗的天色。
宛溪和句溪
夹在楼前，就像是一片明镜，
太阳下山，凤凰和济川二桥
就像落下的彩虹。
傍晚

炊烟缭绕
使桔柚带着苍寒之色，
秋深了，
那些桔柚树也显得更加苍老了。
可是有谁理解我
要独自登上这宣城北楼，
迎着风雨
怀念谢朓公的心情呢？

ON THE NORTHERN TOWER OF XIE TIAO AT XUANCHENG IN AUTUMN

Li Bai

Picturesque is the rivertown;

From hilltop I look up and down.

Two streams seem to flank mirrors bright;

Like rainbows hang bridges left and right.

Grey mist and smoke dye oranges cold;

Chill autumn tints make plane-trees old.

Who knows on Northern Tower high

In the breeze for Xie Tiao I sigh!

送 友 人

李 白

青山横北郭，白水绕东城。
此地一为别，孤蓬万里征。
浮云游子意，落日故人情。
挥手自兹去，萧萧班马鸣。

今 译

簇簇的青山横在北郭，
一道白水，绕过东城。
今天我和你在这里分别，
你就要像孤零零的蓬草
去作那万里远征。
看天上的浮云
来来去去
就好像那出门在外的人
漂泊无定的心意；
望落日的余光
迟迟不退
就好似这依依不舍的
故人的友情。
挥一挥手
你从此便走啦，
这时候
连我们的那匹离了群的马呀
也都不住地
悲鸣！

FAREWELL TO A FRIEND

Li Bai

Green mountains bar the northern sky;

White water girds the eastern town.

Once here we sever, you and I,

You'll drift like lonely thistledown.

With floating cloud you'll float away;

Like parting day I'll part with you.

Waving your hand, you go your way;

Our steeds still neigh: "Adieu, adieu!"

月 夜

杜 甫

今夜鄜州月,闺中只独看。
遥怜小儿女,未解忆长安。
香雾云鬟湿,清辉玉臂寒。
何时倚虚幌,双照泪痕干。

今译

今夜的鄜州的月呀,
在深闺之中
该是只有你独自个儿在看。
我在这远远的地方想
那些可怜的孩子们
恐怕都睡去啦,
而他们
还一点也不知道忆想长安。
呵
夜深啦

露水该湿润了你那云雾一般
散着微香的鬟发吧,
清冷的月光
怕也将侵得你那玉样的
手臂发寒。
不知哪一天
才能相依偎在薄薄的帷帐里,
那时候
让月光,把我俩脸上的
泪痕照干!

A MOONLIT NIGHT

Du Fu

At the moon over Fuzhou which shines bright,

Alone you would gaze in your room tonight.

I'm grieved to think our little children are

Too young to yearn for their father afar.

Your cloudlike hair is moist with dew,it seems;

Your jade-white arms would feel the cold moonbeams.

O when can we stand by the windowside,

Watching the moon with traces of tears dried?

春　望

杜　甫

国破山河在，城春草木深。
感时花溅泪，恨别鸟惊心。
烽火连三月，家书抵万金。
白头搔更短，浑欲不胜簪。

今译

长安虽被攻破
但大好的河山还在，
少有行人
帝城的春天哪
草木已长得很高很高。
花开起来了
然而感伤时事
看到盛开的花朵不禁使人
落泪；
鸟仍在啼唤着呢
可是怨恨别离
听见鸟声，反而更觉得伤心。
呵

战争还没有停息
已度过接连两年的三月，
在这样的日子里
得到一封家书
真抵得上万两黄金。
唉
岁月催人
这满头白发
越搔抓越感到稀少，
稀少得呀
那根白玉的发簪——
简直都要插不住了！

SPRING VIEW

Du Fu

On war-torn land streams flow and mountains stand;

In vernal town grass and weeds are overgrown.

Grieved o'er the years, flowers make us shed tears;

Hating to part, hearing birds breaks our heart.

The beacon fire has gone higher and higher;

Words from household are worth their weight in gold.

I cannot bear to scratch my grizzling hair:

It grows too thin to hold a light hairpin.

月夜忆舍弟

杜 甫

戍鼓断人行，边秋一雁声。
露从今夜白，月是故乡明。
有弟皆分散，无家问死生。
寄书长不达，况乃未休兵。

今译

戍楼上，静夜的更鼓
已经截断了行人来往，
这时候
在秋天的边境上
我听到一阵雁声。
呵
露水呀
从今天夜里，即将变白，
但月亮
却还是那故乡的才最光明。
听着
望着
我不禁想到

为衣为食
几个弟弟
早都东分西散，
到如今
我们都无家可回
也没有地方
去探问他们的死生。
唉
平日里捎书信
都常常不能到达，
更何况
年荒世乱
这普天之下，又正在用兵！

THINKING OF MY BROTHERS ON A MOONLIT NIGHT

Du Fu

War drums break people's journey drear;

A swan honks on autumn frontier.

Dew turns into frost since tonight;

The moon viewed at home would be bright.

I've brothers scattered here or there;

For our life or death none would care.

Letters can't reach where I intend;

Alas!the war's not come to an end.

春夜喜雨

杜 甫

好雨知时节，当春乃发生。
随风潜入夜，润物细无声。
野径云俱黑，江船火独明。
晓看红湿处，花重锦官城。

今译

好的雨水
也像是知道季节，
到了春天
便应时发生。
随着东风
趁着黑夜它悄悄地飘落下来，
滋润着万物
却细微得听不到一点声音。
看吧
雨意正浓
在郊野的小路上

那云彩全已变黑，
这时候
惟有锦江里船上的灯火
还独自在闪着。
呵
等到明天早晨
去看那红湿之处，
花呀
一朵一朵
应该都沉沉实实地
开满这锦官古城！

HAPPY RAIN ON A SPRING NIGHT

Du Fu

Good rain knows its time right;

It will fall when comes spring.

With wind it steals into night;

Mute, it moistens each thing.

O'er wild lanes dark cloud spreads;

In boat a lantern looms.

Dawn sees saturated reds;

The town's heavy with blooms.

喜见外弟又言别

李 益

十年离乱后,长大一相逢。
问姓惊初见,称名忆旧容。
别来沧海事,语罢暮天钟。
明日巴陵道,秋山又几重。

今译

经过十年的离乱之后,
人都长大了
忽然又在此地相逢。
问起姓氏
惊讶这初次的会见,
叫出名字
才忆起旧日的音容。
想我们自从分别以来
经历了多少人事的变迁哪,
叙完话的时候
苍茫的暮色里又响起晚钟。
呵
又要分别啦,
明天
你就在巴陵道了,
我们之间
秋山阻隔
也不知又要有几重?

MEETING AND PARTING WITH MY COUSIN

Li Yi

We parted for ten war-torn years,

Not till grown up do we meet again.

At first I think a stranger appears;

your name reminds me of your face then.

We talk of changeful night and day

Until we hear the evening bell.

Tomorrow you'll go southward way

O'er autumn hills. O fare you well!

赋得古原草送别

白居易

离离原上草，一岁一枯荣。
野火烧不尽，春风吹又生。
远芳侵古道，晴翠接荒城。
又送王孙去，萋萋满别情。

今译

多么茂盛呵
你这大原上的野草，
每过一年
总有一次枯萎，一次茂盛。
原野上燃起的熊熊大火
不能将你彻底烧尽，
春风吹来了
你又再次萌生。

远在天涯的芳草
一直蔓延到眼前的古道，
阳光下天边的绿色
连接着凄凉颓圮的荒城。
我又要
送别友人离去，
青草萋萋
好像也充满了别离的感情。

GRASS ON THE ANCIENT PLAIN— FAREWELL TO A FRIEND

Bai Juyi

Grass on the plain spreads higher and higher;

Year after year it fades and grows.

It can't be burned up by wild fire,

But revives when the spring wind blows.

Its fragrance o'erruns the old way;

Its green invades the ruined town.

To see my friend go far away,

O'erladen with grief, it bends down.

题扬州禅智寺

杜 牧

雨过一蝉噪,飘萧松桂秋。
青苔满阶砌,白鸟故迟留。
暮霭生深树,斜阳下小楼。
谁知竹西路,歌吹是扬州。

今译

小雨过后
忽听到一声蝉噪,
在风中摇曳的松枝桂树
也显出了无限秋意。
那青苔
长满了台阶,
白鸟仍故意地
在寺院里停留。

傍晚的云气
从那茂密的古树林里生起,
夕阳渐渐地
从那一座座小楼边落下了。
呵
谁知道在竹西路,
歌声与器乐声交织着的
便是淮左名都——扬州。

THE WEST BAMBOO TEMPLE AT YANGZHOU

Du Mu

A cicada's loud after rain;

Of sad autumn pine trees complain.

Green moss spreads o'er steps at the gate;

White birds intend to linger late.

From shady woods at dusk clouds rise;

Below a tower sunset dies.

Who knows West Bamboo Road belongs

To rivertown o'erflowing with songs!

晚 晴

李商隐

深居俯夹城,春去夏犹清。
天意怜幽草,人间重晚晴。
并添高阁迥,微注小窗明。
越鸟巢干后,归飞体更轻。

今译

登城眺望着那——
晚晴的古城,
初夏的季节
那景色,使人感到格外清新
宜人。
老天是有意地
在怜惜那些在墙边屋角生长的
小草,

尘世间
人们最看重的是傍晚放晴。
雨后凭高
视野显得十分开阔,
夕阳照射着小小窗户
小窗显得通明通明。
鸟巢干了,鸟羽燥了
飞起来也轻松了。

A SUNNY EVENING AFTER RAIN

Li Shangyin

I look down on town wall from my retreat;

With spring just gone,summer weather is clear.

It's Heaven's will to pity green grass sweet;

The human world holds sunny evening dear.

I can see afar from my tower high;

The parting rays make my small window bright.

The southern birds find their nests again dry;

When they fly back,they feel their bodies light.

商山早行

温庭筠

晨起动征铎,客行悲故乡。
鸡声茅店月,人迹板桥霜。
槲叶落山路,枳花明驿墙。
因思杜陵梦,凫雁满回塘。

今译

清晨
驿站响起催人早行的铃铛,
这时候
行路的人心里不禁悲伤地
怀念起故乡。
阵阵鸡鸣
天边的落日斜照着茅草小店,
行行足迹
清晰地印在那铺满春霜的
板桥上。
枯败的槲叶落满了高山野路,
苍白的枳棘花壳
照亮了驿站的泥墙。
一路上想起
昨夜梦回长安的景况,
还清楚地记得
一群野鸭,落满了堤岸曲折的
池塘。

EARLY DEPARTURE

Wen Tingyun

At dawn I rise and my cab bells begin

To ring, but in thoughts of home I am lost.

The cock crows as the moon sets o'er thatched inn;

Footprints are left on wood bridge paved with frost.

The mountain path is covered with oak leaves;

The post house bright with blooming orange trees.

The dream of my homeland last night still grieves,

Of mallards on the pool playing with geese.

鲁山山行

梅尧臣

适与野情惬,千山高复低。
好峰随处改,幽径独行迷。
霜落熊升树,林空鹿饮溪。
人家在何许?云外一声鸡。

今译

恰恰和我爱好自然景观的习性相宜,
望着那千山万岭有高又有低。
好好的山峰,在眼前忽然又发生奇妙的变化,
幽深的山间小路,连我都会一路迷。
落霜以后,远远可以看到熊在爬树,
整个林子都空了,常会见到那些野鹿在河边饮水。
可是山里的人家在哪里呢?看不到,
这时只听见在云彩外传来一声鸡啼!

ROVING IN THE MOUNTAINS OF DEW

Mei Yaochen

It suits my roving mood

To view hills high and low.

Peaks change their shapes,all good;

So charmed alone I go.

Bears climb on leafless trees;

Deer drink at trackless streams.

Is there a village,please?

Beyond clouds a cock screams.

游大林

周敦颐

三月僧房暖，林花互照明。
路盘层顶上，人在半空行。
水色云含白，禽声谷应清。
天风拂襟袂，缥缈觉身轻。

今译

三月的大林寺里
十分温暖，
树林里的花
互相照映，格外分明。
那些道路
盘旋到一层的山顶之上，
人哪
就好像在半空里行走。
山上潭水清澈

云彩像被含在水里，显得十分
清净，
鸟雀的啼鸣在山里回响
显得格外清晰。
天上的风吹拂着
衣襟和衣袖，
飘飘摇摇，隐隐约约
使人感到身子都有点发轻。

VISITING DALIN TEMPLE

Zhou Dunyi

The temple is warm in spring days;

Bright flowers bloom beyond compare.

Atop the mountain wind pathways;

People walk as if in mid-air.

Clouds mirrored in water look white;

The vale's echo with birds sounds clear.

My sleeves waft in wind as in flight;

I feel my body light and freer.

雨 过

周紫芝

池面过小雨，树腰生夕阳。
云分一山翠，风与数荷香。
素月自有约，绿瓜初可尝。
鸂鶒莫飞去，留此伴新凉。

今 译

池塘的水面上
飘过了一阵小雨，
在树林的半腰里
露出一片夕阳。
雨后，还在飘动的云彩
分得了一座山的青翠之色，
轻风徐来
好像与那几朵初开的荷花一样
飘香。

明洁的月亮，缓缓升起
就好像早有约会，
那些还绿着的瓜
似乎刚刚可以品尝。
鸂鶒呵
且不要飞走，
留在这里
陪伴我度此新凉。

AFTER RAIN

Zhou Zizhi

Over the pool lightly it rained;

A setting sun grows beside trees.

With mountain's green white clouds are stained;

Fragrant with lotus blows the breeze.

The melon fresh is good to taste;

On promise will rise the moon clear.

Herons, don't fly away in haste!

Stay and enjoy the coolness here!

白　菊

许廷铩

正得西方气，来开篱下花。
素心常耐冷，晚节本无瑕。
质傲清霜色，香含秋露华。
白衣何处去，载酒问陶家。

今译

那白菊
正得了西风的秋气，
它吹开了
那篱下的花。
素洁的心
常常耐得寒冷，
惟有白菊仍抱枝开放
正如人的晚节，本来就没有
斑瑕。

品质傲然
显出一派清霜的颜色，
香里含着
秋天霜露的精华。
呵
那穿白衣的人——王弘
要到什么地方去？
一定载着酒——
来访问我这陶渊明的家！

TO WHITE CHRYSANTHEMUMS

Xu Tingheng

The western air can mold

In bloom the hedgeside flowers.

Your pure heart stands the cold;

You're spotless in late hours:

Proud against frost and snow,

Fragrant with autumn dew.

Where will your white dress go?

Wine is the poet's due.

黄 鹤 楼

崔 颢

昔人已乘黄鹤去，此地空余黄鹤楼。
黄鹤一去不复返，白云千载空悠悠。
晴川历历汉阳树，芳草萋萋鹦鹉洲。
日暮乡关何处是，烟波江上使人愁。

今译

从前那位登仙的人
已经驾着黄鹤飞走，
如今在这里
只剩下了一座黄鹤楼。
黄鹤一去啊
不再回返，
人们能看到的
惟有那千年飘浮不尽的白云
还在楼头荡荡悠悠。
呵
眼前水道分明
远远望去
清清楚楚、历历在目的是
汉阳树，
附近绿色撩人
那芳草萋萋的地方
便是黄祖枉杀祢衡的鹦鹉洲。
看
天已经傍晚
请问
我的故乡在哪里？
默对着这江上起伏的烟波呀
真使人不胜忧愁！

YELLOW CRANE TOWER

Cui Hao

The sage on yellow crane was gone amid clouds white.

To what avail is Yellow Crane Tower left here?

Once gone, the yellow crane will ne'er on earth alight;

Only white clouds still float in vain from year to year.

By sunlit river trees can be count'd one by one;

On Parrot Islet sweet green grass grows fast and thick.

Where is my native land beyond the setting sun?

The mist-veiled waves of the Han River make me homesick.

闻官军收河南河北

杜 甫

剑外忽传收蓟北,初闻涕泪满衣裳。
却看妻子愁何在,漫卷诗书喜欲狂。
白日放歌须纵酒,青春作伴好还乡。
即从巴峡穿巫峡,便下襄阳向洛阳。

今译

在剑门关外
忽然传说
我军已收复河北,
乍一听到
高兴得我鼻涕眼泪
淌满了衣裳。
回过头,看看妻子
似乎还有一些什么忧愁?
胡乱地收拾着诗书
我不禁欢喜得都要发狂。
呵
在这样的日子里
应该放声歌唱

也应该尽情喝酒,
明媚的春光
伴随我
带着家小
和他们一路还乡。
呵
说话就要动身了
我将沿着大江
穿过巫峡,再经由巴峡,
等顺水到了襄阳
便转走旱路,奔向那东都洛阳!

RECAPTURE OF THE REGIONS NORTH AND SOUTH OF THE YELLOW RIVER

Du Fu

'Tis said the Northern Gate is recaptured of late;

When the news reach my ears,my gown is wet with tears.

Staring at my wife's face,of grief I find no trace;

Rolling up my verse books,my joy like madness looks.

White-haired as I am,still I'd sing and drink my fill;

With verdure spring's aglow,it's time we homeward go.

We shall sail all the way through Three Gorges in a day;

Going down to Xiangyang,we'll come up to Luoyang.

江　村

杜　甫

清江一曲抱村流，长夏江村事事幽。
自去自来堂上燕，相亲相近水中鸥。
老妻画纸为棋局，稚子敲针作钓钩。
多病所需惟药物，微躯此外更何求？

今译

清清的锦江
弯弯一曲
抱着村庄在流，
漫长的夏日
在这临江村庄里边
事事都显得那般舒适清幽。
看
自来自去的
是那堂上的双双小燕，
相亲相近的
是那水上的对对白鸥。

闲暇无事
老妻展开纸
画着棋局，
没忧没虑
孩子敲弯钢针
在做着钓钩。
呵
年老多病
需要的惟有药物，
除此之外
还有什么可求？

THE RIVERSIDE VILLAGE

Du Fu

The winding clear river around the village flows;

We pass the long summer by riverside with ease.

The swallows freely come in and freely out go;

The gulls on water snuggle each other as they please.

My wife draws lines on paper to make a chessboard;

My son knocks a needle into a fishing hook.

Ill, I need only medicine I can afford.

What else do I need for myself in humble nook?

蜀 相

杜 甫

蜀相祠堂何处寻，锦官城外柏森森。
映阶碧草自春色，隔叶黄鹂空好音。
三顾频烦天下计，两朝开济老臣心。
出师未捷身先死，长使英雄泪满襟。

今译

诸葛丞相的祠堂
要到什么地方去找寻？
人们告诉我说：
"就在锦官城外
那里古柏森森！"
呵
人迹罕到
照映石阶的碧草
自然形成一片春天的景色；
无人欣赏
躲藏在密叶深处的黄鹂
也空自在婉转着动人的娇音。
忆昔当年
风雪南归
三顾茅庐
一再劳烦的
乃是那安邦济世的天下大计；
终于出山
帮助先主开基立业
辅佐后主撑持危局
完全表现了
你这两代老臣的一片耿耿忠心。
但
令人遗憾的是——
北伐曹魏，
兵据五丈原
胜负尚未决出
你在万马千军中便身先病死，
千载以来
每当想到这些
又怎么能不使那些英雄志士们
——泪满衣襟！

THE PREMIER OF SHU

Du Fu

Where is the famous Premier's Temple to be found?

Outside the Town of Brocade with cypress around.

In vain before the steps reminding of spring grows

grass green and long

And amid the leaves golden orioles sing their song.

The king visited him for advice thrice and again;

He served the kingdom heart and soul during two

reigns.

But he died before he'd accomplished his career.

How could heroes not wet their sleeves with tear

on tear!

左迁至蓝关示侄孙湘

韩　愈

一封朝奏九重天，夕贬潮州路八千。
欲为圣明除弊事，肯将衰朽惜残年！
云横秦岭家何在？雪拥蓝关马不前。
知汝远来应有意，好收吾骨瘴江边。

今译

清晨
我把一封奏章
呈上了那金銮宝殿，
傍晚
被贬去潮阳
路程呵，竟有八千。
本来
谏迎佛骨
乃是为了给皇上
铲除那些有害的政事，
所以
虽然明明知道将会被怪罪
而我
又怎么敢以衰朽多病的身体
爱惜那风里残烛一般的晚年？

唉
当望到云彩横在秦岭的时候
我不禁在心里问起：我的家乡
在哪？
而那一天纷纷扬扬的大雪
正拥塞着蓝关
连我的马呀
也已经驻足不前！
湘子呵
我知道你远道而来
应该是，怀有深意，
你不过是
为了收拾我这把老骨头呵
——在那充满着瘴气的大江边！

WRITTEN FOR MY GRANDNEPHEW AT THE BLUE PASS

Han Yu

At dawn to Royal Court a proposal was made;

At dusk I'm banished eight thousand li away.

To undo the misdeeds I would have given aid.

Dare I have spared myself with powers in decay?

The Ridge veiled in barred clouds, my home cannot be seen;

The Blue Pass clad in snow, my horse won't forward go.

You have come from afar and I know what you mean:

To bury my old bones where the misty waters flow.

酬乐天扬州初逢席上见赠

刘禹锡

巴山楚水凄凉地，二十三年弃置身。
怀旧空吟闻笛赋，到乡翻似烂柯人。
沉舟侧畔千帆过，病树前头万木春。
今日听君歌一曲，暂凭杯酒长精神。

今译

巴地多山
楚地多水
而这一带所有的地方
都不过使人感到荒远和凄凉，
二十三载
今年在这里
明年又那方
我不过是一个为朝廷贬斥在外的人。
每当想起一些知心好友已零落殆尽
我便吟诵向秀闻笛时写的那篇《思旧赋》，
而回到这地近苏州的故乡来
反而成了神话中写的那个——
手里的斧柄烂掉了的人。

呵
我就像一艘沉舟
在我的身旁
那些得势的新贵们
好似千帆竞渡，飞驰而过，
我又像一棵病树
在我的面前
那些得势的新贵们
恰如充满生机的万木在争春。
唉
在今天的酒席宴前
我聆听着你"把箸击盘"
为我歌唱的那一曲
很感谢你的宽慰——乐天
但愿我能凭借着这杯美酒
满怀激情，重新振作起精神！

REPLY TO BAI JUYI WHOM I MET FOR THE FIRST TIME AT A BANQUET IN YANGZHOU

Liu Yuxi

O Western mountains and Southern streams desolate,

Where I, an exile, lived for twenty years and three!

To mourn for my departed friends I come too late;

In native land I look but like human debris.

A thousand sails pass by the side of sunken ship;

Ten thousand flowers bloom ahead of injured tree.

Today I hear you chant the praises of friendship;

I wish this cup of wine might well inspirit me.

钱塘湖春行

白居易

孤山寺北贾亭西,水面初平云脚低。
几处早莺争暖树,谁家新燕啄春泥。
乱花渐欲迷人眼,浅草才能没马蹄。
最爱湖东行不足,绿杨阴里白沙堤。

今译

在孤山那些寺院北边的
贾亭以西,
湖面刚刚漫平
云彩呀,飘得很低很低。
有几处地方
初飞的黄莺儿
蹦上跳下,在争夺着
向阳的树;
也不知是谁家
新归来的小燕子
正在水边,啄着春泥。
杂花开得繁盛起来
渐渐地要迷乱人们的双眼;
长得不高的小草绿绿茸茸
刚能没过那马蹄。
但我最爱的还是湖东
总感到它叫人游走个不够,
总叫人游走个不够呵
——那绿杨浓阴里的一带白沙
长堤!

LAKE QIANTANG IN SPRING

Bai Juyi

West of Pavilion Jia and north of Lonely Hill,

O'er level water surface clouds are hanging low.

Disputing for sunny trees, early orioles trill;

Pecking in vernal mud, young swallows come and go.

A riot of blooms begin to dazzle the eye;

Amid short grass the horsehoofs can barely be seen.

I love best the east of the lake under the sky:

The bank paved with white sand is shaded by willows green.

无 题

李商隐

相见时难别亦难，东风无力百花残。
春蚕到死丝方尽，蜡炬成灰泪始干。
晓镜但愁云鬓改，夜吟应觉月光寒。
蓬山此去无多路，青鸟殷勤为探看。

今译

相见一次很难
分别开来也是个难，
东风无力再吹了
一切花朵呀，已经都凋残。
但——
春蚕只有到死的时候
那丝，方能吐尽，
蜡烛呵
只有成灰的时候
那泪，才会滴干！
珍重些吧
清晨对镜
令人忧愁的
是你那乌云一般的鬓发
悄悄变改，
深夜里
在月光下独吟
亲爱的
你该小心
不要让那身子骨儿受寒。
呵
蓬莱仙山
距离这里
本来并没有——多少道路，
传递消息的青鸟呵
求你殷勤些吧——
能常常去为我，把你探看！

TO ONE UNNAMED

Li Shangyin

It's difficult for us to meet and hard to part;

The east wind is too weak to revive flowers dead.

Spring silkworm till its death spins silk from lovesick heart;

A candle but when burned up has no tears to shed.

At dawn I'm grieved to think your mirrored hair turns grey;

At night you would feel cold while I croon by moonlight.

To the three fairy mountains it's not a long way.

Would the blue birds oft fly to see you on the height!

山中寡妇

杜荀鹤

夫因兵死守蓬茅，麻苎衣衫鬓发焦。
桑柘废来犹纳税，田园荒后尚征苗。
时挑野菜和根煮，旋斫生柴带叶烧。
任是深山更深处，也应无计避征徭。

今译

丈夫因为战乱当兵死了，
她只好独自一人守着茅屋，
穿的是粗糙的麻布衣裳，鬓发
已经都枯焦。
种桑柘的田地已经荒废
可是还要纳捐上税，
田园都荒芜了以后
官家还在征苗。
时时挖采野菜
带着根儿来煮，
转过身来
破些生柴
带着叶子来烧。
即使是住在
深山老林的那最深的地方，
也还是没有办法
躲避那些赋税和劳役！

A WIDOW LIVING IN THE MOUNTAIN

Du Xunhe

Her husband killed in war, she lives in a thatched hut,

Wearing coarse hemper clothes and a flaxen hair.

She should pay taxes though mulberries were down cut,

And before harvest though fields and gardens lie bare.

She has to eat wild herbs together with their root

And burn as fuel leafy branches from the tree.

However deep she hides in mountains as a brute,

From oppressive taxes she can never be free.

贫 女

秦韬玉

蓬门未识绮罗香，拟托良媒益自伤。
谁爱风流高格调，共怜时世俭梳妆。
敢将十指夸针巧，不把双眉斗画长。
苦恨年年压金线，为他人作嫁衣裳。

今 译

出生蓬门
从未知晓
绫罗绸缎的馨香，
想托个良媒
却更加感到
内心的悲伤。
有谁爱
风流潇洒的
高尚的格调，
共惜时世艰难
像她一样
打扮得朴素大方。
她呀
敢用十指
夸耀针线做得精巧，
不愿同人们
在画眉上
去争短论长。
最可恨的是，年年岁岁
都在辛勤地
刺绣着金线，
却不过是
为了旁人
在做嫁时的衣裳！

A POOR MAID

Qin Taoyu

In thatched hut I know not fragrant silk and brocade;

To be married I can't find a good go-between.

Who would love an uncommon fashion though self-made?

All pity my simple toilet and humble mien.

I dare boast my fingers' needlework without peer,

But I won't vie with maidens painting eyebrows long.

I regret to stitch golden thread from year to year

But to make wedding gowns which to others belong.

戏答元珍

欧阳修

春风疑不到天涯，二月山城未见花。
残雪压枝犹有橘，冻雷惊笋欲抽芽。
夜闻归雁生乡思，病入新年感物华。
曾是洛阳花下客，野芳虽晚不须嗟。

今译

那温软的春风
令人疑惑它
吹不到这荒远的天涯，
不是吗
都进了三月
在这座山城里
竟还没有看见开花。
残余的霜雪
仍压在枝头
那上边尚挂有剩下的柚桔，
可是
解冻的雷声
却好像惊醒了笋儿

它们都要抽出嫩芽。
昨晚
曾听到北归的雁鸣
我不禁生起了一片乡思，
带着疾病
又进入新的一年
让人有感于物华。
我曾是
洛阳牡丹的花下之客，
在这偏僻的乡野地方
花儿开得虽然较晚
却也用不着长吁短嗟！

REPLY TO YUAN ZHEN

Ouyang Xiu

I am afraid here the vernal wind will not blow;

In second moon no hillside flowers have come out.

But oranges grow on trees bowed with lingering snow,

And bamboo shoots startled by frozen thunder sprout.

I am homesick to hear homing wild geese at night;

Though in bad health, I feel the reviving new year.

We had our day in Capital of Flowers bright.

Why should we lament when wild flowers come late here!

偶 成

程 颢

闲来无事不从容,睡觉东窗日已红。
万物静观皆自得,四时佳兴与人同。
道通天地有形外,思入风云变态中。
富贵不淫贫贱乐,男儿到此是豪雄。

今译

空闲时节
对一切事物,都无不
从从容容,
一觉醒来
才感到,东窗上已太阳通红。
静观万物
无不自由自在,都那样
自得其乐,
一年四季

那美好的景色
我与人们的兴致也都相同。
道体无所不在
贯穿超越于天地有形物之外,
思维深入宇宙的
风云变化当中。
男子汉大丈夫能做到
富贵不淫、贫贱仍然自得其乐,
那便算得是真正的豪杰英雄!

A RANDOM POEM

Cheng Hao

There's nothing I do but with ease when I'm at leisure;
A wake, I find east window reddened in sunlight.
Nature contemplated calmly has its own pleasure;
I enjoy four seasons with all men in delight.
Law is formless but reigns over heaven and earth;
Thoughts assume various shapes and change like wind and cloud.
Wealth can't seduce me;poverty won't reduce mirth:
A man who attains this may be a hero proud.

游山西村

陆　游

莫笑农家腊酒浑，丰年留客足鸡豚。
山重水复疑无路，柳暗花明又一村。
箫鼓追随春社近，衣冠简朴古风存。
从今若许闲乘月，拄杖无时夜叩门。

今译

不要笑话
农民家里
那头年腊月酿造的酒浑浊，
丰收之年
挽留客人
有非常丰盛的
——菜肴。
山哪一重一重
水呀一道一道
真使我怀疑——
那前面已经没有了去路，
可是
柳色深绿
花儿艳红
忽然在眼前又出现了一座
小山村。
人们吹着箫
打着鼓
成群结队
来来往往
是因为春社的日子已经临近，
衣冠穿戴
都朴朴实实
看上去那古时的遗风遗俗犹存。
呵
从今往后
如果能够允许我
在有闲的时候
乘着月色漫长，
我一定
拄着拐杖
时时地——
来叩你们家的柴门。

THE WESTERN MOUNTAIN VILLAGE

Lu You

Say not the farmers have but last year's muddy wine!

After harvest you're offered pork and chicken fine.

Beyond the hills and rills the path seems lost to sight;

A village's seen 'mid shady willows and flowers bright.

Flute songs and drumbeats announce vernal sacrifice;

Simple dress preserves ancient way of living nice.

If I'm allowed to come at leisure by moonlight,

Cane in hand, I'd come anytime to knock at night.

书 愤

陆 游

早岁那知世事艰,中原北望气如山。
楼船夜雪瓜洲渡,铁马秋风大散关。
塞上长城空自许,镜中衰鬓已先斑。
出师一表真名世,千载谁堪伯仲间!

今译

早在青年和壮年
哪里知道人生世事的艰辛?
只要登高
北望沦陷的中原土地
满心杀敌的愤慨之气
便会涌积如山。
我常想到
从前
我们的军队
曾驾着高大的战船
飘雪的夜晚
抗战在瓜洲古渡;
我也难忘
从戎南郑
跨着披甲的战马
迎着萧瑟的秋风
戍守在大散关前!
可是如今
把自己看成是国家长城的志望
已经完全落空,
对着明镜
不觉地
早就两鬓斑斑。
呵
那坚持北伐的
诸葛亮的《出师表》
真可以说是名传后世,
千载以来
谁能同他相比
有如不相上下的兄弟!

INDIGNATION

Lu You

How could I know the hard times in my early days?
Looking north, I heave up and down like mountain ways.
Warships crossed Melon Ferry on a snowy night;
Armored steeds ran in autumn breeze to border height.
In vain I'd be a " Great Wall "to bar the foe's way;
Before its time my hair in the mirror turns grey.
The premier's fame is widespread even on frontiers.
Who can boast to equal him for a thousand years?

临安春雨初霁

陆 游

世味年来薄似纱，谁令骑马客京华？
小楼一夜听春雨，深巷明朝卖杏花。
矮纸斜行闲作草，晴窗细乳戏分茶。
素衣莫起风尘叹，犹及清明可到家。

今译

一切人情世味
在近年以来
已使人感到轻薄如纱，
可是
又谁令你
骑着一匹老马
作客在这势利的京华？
呵
在这座小楼里
昨晚上
听了一夜春雨，
第二天早晨
那深巷之中
便有人在叫卖杏花。

闲居无事
我只好展开短纸
在上面练习大草，
百无聊赖
也惟有坐在晴朗的窗前
戏耍着品叶分茶。
呵，一身素洁
用不着
由于饱染风尘而感慨兴叹，
因为
还赶得及
在清明之前
便可以回到三山村——
我自己的家！

A SUNNY SPRING DAY AFTER A RAINY NIGHT IN THE CAPITAL

Lu You

The world tastes chilly like thin gauze in recent years.

Who tells you to ride in the capital like Peers?

Last night in the attic I heard the vernal rain;

Next day apricot blooms will be sold in deep lane.

On short paper I try my calligraphy free;

Under the window I enjoy my bubbled tea.

Do not complain your white dress is soiled in the breeze!

You may go home before Mourning Day if you please.

过零丁洋

文天祥

辛苦遭逢起一经,干戈寥落四周星。
山河破碎风飘絮,身世浮沉雨打萍。
惶恐滩头说惶恐,零丁洋里叹零丁。
人生自古谁无死,留取丹心照汗青。

今译

辛勤刻苦
遭逢际遇
都是起于一经的精通,
奔走国事
在战争当中
寥寥落落地,竟度过了四年光阴。
山河破碎
就像那在风里飘飞着的
散乱的柳絮,
动荡不宁
个人的身世浮沉
就如被冷雨淋打着的水上浮萍。

回想当日
在惶恐滩头
曾讲说过险流恶浪的惶恐,
到而今
路过零丁洋畔
不禁叹息着自己的孤苦零丁。
呵
人生不过百年
自古以来
谁又能没有个死?
即使如此
还是要留得一片爱国忠心
永远照耀在史册之中!

THE LONELY OCEAN

Wen Tianxiang

I studied hard the classics,rose to serve the state

And fought against odds for four years with might and main.

Like wafting willow-down is war-torn country's fate;

It sinks or swims as duckweeds beaten by the rain.

The frightful Reef once frightened us to lose our breath;

The Lonely Ocean makes us feel lonely and heave sighs.

Since olden days there is no man but suffers death;

I'd leave a loyal heart which history glorifies.

赴戍登程口占示家人

林则徐

力微任重久神疲,再竭衰庸定不支。
苟利国家生死以,岂因祸福避趋之。
谪居正是君恩厚,养拙刚于戍卒宜。
戏与山妻谈故事,试吟断送老头皮。

今译

力量微薄,任务重大
长久以来,已使我痛感
力尽神疲,
再加上竭力背负重担
这软弱的身体早感到
单薄难支。
我常想
若能利国利家
无论是生死,都当毫无顾忌,
哪能因为有祸有福
就躲避灾害而去追逐名利!
流放边疆
正意味着皇上的恩情深而且重,
安于笨拙,发配伊犁
沦为戍卒倒也非常之相宜。
该上路了
与老妻且谈谈过往的那些旧事,
你不要悲伤
且尝试着像宋代杨朴妻子那样
吟诵一首"断送老头皮"!

BEFORE GOING INTO EXILE

Lin Zexu

Weary for long with feeble strength and duty great,

Mediocrity exhausted, could I not sink low?

I'd risk life and brave death to do good to the state.

Could I but for myself seek weal and avoid woe?

The banishment just shows the royal favor high;

My border service is good to do what I can.

I tease my wife with a story of days gone by:

Why not try to chant verse to see off your old man?

黄海舟中日人索句
并见日俄战争地图

秋　瑾

万里乘风去复来，只身东海挟春雷。
忍看图画移颜色，肯使江山付劫灰！
浊酒不销忧国泪，救时应仗出群才。
拼将十万头颅血，须把乾坤力挽回。

今译

乘风破浪，万里汪洋
去了又来，
只身一人，在东海之上
挟着革命的春雷而归。
怎么忍心看着地图
改变了颜色？
又怎么肯使大好河山
遭到毁坏变成劫灰？

浊酒数杯
销溶不了忧国的悲泪，
拯救时危
要仰仗着出众的英才。
豁出去拼杀
抛洒千万头颅和热血，
一定要让颠倒的乾坤
再颠倒过来！

LINES WRITTEN AT THE REQUEST OF A JAPANESE IN A SHIP ON THE YELLOW SEA AFTER SEEING A MAP OF THE RUSSO-JAPANESE WAR

Qiu Jin

Riding the wind, I crossed and recross the East Sea;

Alone I feel vernal thunder stir within me.

How could I bear to see our map changing its hue?

Could I suffer our land turned to ashes in view?

With muddy wine we can't wipe away bitter tears;

To turn the tide we need outstanding pioneers.

If one hundred thousand men fear not to shed blood,

We'd move heaven and earth to stem the rising flood.

江 南

汉乐府

江南可采莲，
莲叶何田田。
鱼戏莲叶间：
鱼戏莲叶东，
鱼戏莲叶西，
鱼戏莲叶南，
鱼戏莲叶北。

今译

江南大好时光
这时正好采摘莲蓬，
莲叶呀
浮在水上，
那么茂密，连成一片。
鱼儿
游戏在莲叶之间：
鱼戏耍着
莲叶忽而向东，
鱼戏耍着
莲叶忽而又向西。
鱼戏耍着
莲叶忽而向南，
鱼戏耍着
莲叶忽而又向北。

THE SOUTHERN RIVERSHORE

Music Bureau

Gather lotus seed all the way!

How joyfully lotus leaves sway!

Among the lotus leaves fish play:

East of the lotus leaves fish play;

West of the lotus leaves fish play;

South of the lotus leaves fish play;

North of the lotus leaves fish play.

长 歌 行

汉乐府

青青园中葵,朝露待日晞。
阳春布德泽,万物生光辉。
常恐秋节至,焜黄华叶衰。
百川东到海,何时复西归?
少壮不努力,老大徒伤悲。

今译

葱葱郁郁的
园子里的向日葵,
太阳出来的时候,
早晨的露水会被晒干。
阳春三月里
因为有了春暖,一切才会充满生机。
常常会担忧
秋天时节又悄悄来到,
一切都枯黄了
叶子也都凋落。
千百江河
都流向了东洋大海,
可什么时候
它们才再西归?
青春年少时
不肯奋发上进,
等到老了
只好在那里徒自伤悲!

A SLOW SONG

Music Bureau

The mallow in the garden green in hue

Awaits the sun to dry the morning dew.

The radiant spring spreads its nourishing light;

All living things become then fresh and bright.

They dread the coming of the autumn drear

When leaves turn yellow and red flowers sere.

A hundred streams flow eastward to the sea.

When to return to the west will they be free?

If one does not make good use of his youth,

In vain will he pass his old age in ruth.

赠从弟

刘 桢

其 二

亭亭山上松,瑟瑟谷中风。
风声一何盛,松枝一何劲。
冰霜正惨凄,终岁常端正。
岂不罹凝寒,松柏有本性。

今译

孤高挺拔的
山上的松,
山谷中吹着
瑟瑟的风。
风呵
是多么的凶猛,
松枝呵
你又是多么的坚劲。
冰和霜

带着凛冽将你袭击,
但山上的松
却终身都刚直端正。
难道你
不曾遭到严寒的侵逼?
不是的
是因为——
松和柏自有耐寒的坚贞本性。

TO MY COUSIN

Liu Zhen

The pine on hill-top towers high;

The winds in the val sough and sigh.

However violent they may be,

Unshakable stands the pine-tree.

Though ice and frost look sad and drear,

The tree stands straight throughout the year.

Does it not fear the biting cold?

It stands on its own as of old.

野田黄雀行

曹 植

高树多悲风,海水扬其波。
利剑不在掌,结友何须多!
不见篱间雀,见鹞自投罗?
罗家见雀喜,少年见雀悲。
拔剑捎罗网,黄雀得飞飞。
飞飞摩苍天,来下谢少年。

今译

高大的松树
常常招惹凄厉的风,
大海辽阔
往往掀起险恶的浪波。
锋利的宝剑
没有握在自己手里,
交结朋友
又何须太多?
你没见到过篱间的
那群黄雀吗?
看见鹞鹰
自己竟陷入网罗。
见到雀儿
张网的猎人十分欢喜。
少年人见到雀儿
却感到十分伤悲。
拔出宝剑
削除罗网,
黄雀得以高高地轻快地飞。
轻快地
高飞到天上去,
然后飞下来
感谢救助他的那位少年。

SONG OF THE YELLOW BIRD

Cao Zhi

Tall trees are saddened by the breeze;

Strong breezes raise waves in the seas.

Without a sharp sword in the hand,

Why make many friends in the land?

Seeing eagles, the hedgeside bird

Falls in the net, have you not heard?

Seeing it trapped, the hunter's glad;

Seeing it caught, a young man's sad.

The youth cuts with his sword the net

So that the bird away may get.

It flies away to scrape the sky

And thanks the young man from on high.

归园田居

陶渊明

其 三

种豆南山下，草盛豆苗稀。
晨兴理荒秽，带月荷锄归。
道狭草木长，夕露沾我衣。
衣沾不足惜，但使愿无违。

今译

种植豆苗
在南山之下，
杂草很茂密
豆苗却很稀少。
早晨起来
去锄那些杂草，
黄昏
月亮出来
才扛着锄头而归。

小路狭窄
草木丛生，
晚上的露水
沾湿了我的衣裳。
沾湿衣裳
并不值得可惜，
只要我隐居归耕的志愿
能不违背！

RETURN TO NATURE

Tao Yuanming

I sow my beans'neath Southern Hill;

Bean shoots are lost where weeds o'ergrow.

I weed at dawn though early still;

I plod home with my moonlit hoe.

The path is narrow and grass tall;

With evening dew my clothes are wet.

I don't heed my wet clothes at all;

If only my desire be met.

宿五松山下荀媪家

李　白

我宿五松下，寂寥无所欢。
田家秋作苦，邻女夜舂寒。
跪进雕胡饭，月光明素盘。
令人惭漂母，三谢不能餐。

今译

我借宿在五松山下的
荀姓老婆婆家中，
心里感到
十分的苦闷和孤单。
农民
秋天的劳作十分辛苦，
邻家的女儿
舂着米不管秋夜的寒风。

房主人跪着
送给我菰米饭，
月光照着
明洁朴素的餐盘。
这令我想起韩信
不禁感到在漂母面前有些惭愧，
所以再三感谢
而不能进餐。

PASSING ONE NIGHT IN AN OLD WOMAN'S HUT AT THE FOOT OF MOUNT FIVE PINES

Li Bai

I lodge under the five pine trees;

Lonely, I feel not quite at ease.

Peasants work hard in autumn old;

Husking rice at night, the maid's cold.

Wild rice is offered on her knees;

The plate in moonlight seems to freeze.

I'm overwhelmed with gratitude.

Do I deserve the hard-earned food?

望 岳

杜 甫

岱宗夫如何，齐鲁青未了。
造化钟神秀，阴阳割昏晓。
荡胸生层云，决眦入归鸟。
会当凌绝顶，一览众山小。

今 译

五岳独尊的泰山
到底是个什么模样？
论气象，覆盖两州
横走齐州纵走鲁
仍是蜿蜿蜒蜒，郁郁葱葱
没有个完也没有个了！
就好像天地之间的神奇和秀丽
都在这里聚集，
一面背阴
一面朝阳
在那高峰山岭的南北
竟分割出昏夜和拂晓。

激荡胸怀的
是时刻在滋长着的
那一层一层的云雾，
极目望去
都能看到在远远的地方
有一只一只回巢的飞鸟。
呵
总有一天
我要攀登上绝顶，
看着那脚下的群山
是那样的低微和渺小！

GAZING ON MOUNT TAI

Du Fu

O peak of peaks, how high it stands!

One boundless green o'erspreads two States.

A marvel done by Nature's hands,

O'er light and shade it dominates.

Clouds rise therefrom and lave my breast;

My eyes are strained to see birds fleet.

Try to ascend the mountain's crest!

It dwarfs all peaks under your feet.

游子吟

孟 郊

慈母手中线，游子身上衣。
临行密密缝，意恐迟迟归。
谁言寸草心，报得三春晖！

今译

慈母手里在做着的针线活，
是远走他乡的孩子身上的衣裳；
临行的时候
她密密匝匝地缝，
那心意是——
怕孩子飘泊在外边迟迟不归。
呵，
谁说那微细的小草儿的一点绿意，
能够报答得了
这整个春天里的太阳的光辉？

SONG OF THE PARTING SON

Meng Jiao

From the threads a mother's hand weaves

A gown for parting son is made,

Sewn stitch by stitch before he leaves

For fear his return be delayed.

Such kindness as young grass receives

From the warm sun can be repaid?

敕 勒 歌

北朝民歌

敕勒川，阴山下。
天似穹庐，笼盖四野。
天苍苍，野茫茫，
风吹草低见牛羊。

今译

广阔的敕勒川，
绵绵延延
在阴山之下。
天哪
就好像是我们的穹庐，
笼盖在这无边的
莽莽苍苍的四野。
天呵
苍苍茫茫，
四野呵
莽莽苍苍，
风吹来
草低下
便现出了那成群的牛和羊！

A SHEPHERD'S SONG

Anonymous

At the foot of the hill,

By the side of the rill,

The grassland stretches 'neath the firmament tranquil.

The boundless grassland lies

Beneath the boundless skies.

When the winds blow

And grass bends low,

My sheep and cattle will emerge before your eyes.

春江花月夜

张若虚

春江潮水连海平,海上明月共潮生。
滟滟随波千万里,何处春江无月明。
江流宛转绕芳甸,月照花林皆似霰。
空里流霜不觉飞,汀上白沙看不见。
江天一色无纤尘,皎皎空中孤月轮。
江畔何人初见月?江月何年初照人?

今译

春天,江潮连着江潮
远远望去,漫平漫平,
海上的明月
和潮水一同升起。
水波流荡
闪着光亮,望去有千里万里,
试问
什么地方的春江之上
没有月明?
江流呵
委委婉婉,弯弯曲曲
绕过芳草萋萋的原野、荒甸,
月亮呵
照映着开花的树林
开花的树林,就像凝结着一层雪霰。
半空里,飘动着的月色

就像流霜一样,不觉得它们在飞,
江边小洲上的白沙呵
一点也看不见。
大江和长天,浑为一色
没有一点灰尘,
天空之中
孤孤单单
只有明月一轮。
呵
在大江之畔
什么人
最初看见江上的明月?
大江之上的明月
又从什么时候
才开始照人?

A MOONLIT NIGHT ON THE SPRING RIVER

Zhang Ruoxu

In spring the river rises as high as the sea,

And with the river's tide uprises the moon bright.

She follows the rolling waves for ten thousand li,

Where'er the river flows, there overflows her light.

The river winds around the fragrant islets where

All flowers in moonlight look like snow, plum or peach.

You cannot tell moonbeams from hoar frost in the air,

Nor from the white sand upon the Farewell Beach.

No dust has stained the water blending with the skies;

A lonely wheellike moon shines brilliant far and wide.

Who did by the riverside see the moon first rise?

When did the moon first see a man by riverside?

人生代代无穷已，江月年年只相似。
不知江月待何人，但见长江送流水。
白云一片去悠悠，青枫浦上不胜愁。
谁家今夜扁舟子？何处相思明月楼？
可怜楼上月徘徊，应照离人妆镜台。
玉户帘中卷不去，捣衣砧上拂还来。

今译

人生呵
一代一代
没有个穷尽，
江上的明月
一年一年
始终相似。
也不知那江上的明月
在等待什么人？
只见那长江
终日漂送着东去的流水。
白云哪
去去来来
一片一片
荡荡悠悠，
青枫浦上的人哪
那心里
充满了说不清的忧愁。
今夜
飘泊在江船上的
是谁家的游子？
相思的人哪
又是站在什么地方的楼头？
明月呵
正在楼头徘徊，
应该照着——
她那梳妆的镜台。
明月呵
透进窗帘
卷也卷不去，
明月呵
倾泻在捣衣石上
拂去又来。

Ah, generations have come and passed away;

From year to year the moon looks alike, old and new.

We do not know for whom tonight she sheds her ray,

But hear the river say to its water adieu.

Away, away is sailing a single cloud white;

On Farewell Beach are pining away maples green.

Where is the wanderer sailing his boat tonight?

Who, pining away, on the moonlit rails would lean?

Alas! The moon is lingering over her tower;

It should have seen her dressing table all alone.

She may roll curtains up and light is in her bower;

She may wash but moonbeams still remain on the stone.

此时相望不相闻，愿逐月华流照君。
鸿雁长飞光不度，鱼龙潜跃水成文。
昨夜闲潭梦落花，可怜春半不还家。
江水流春去欲尽，江潭落月复西斜。
斜月沉沉藏海雾，碣石潇湘无限路。
不知乘月几人归，落月摇情满江树。

今译

这时候
互相望着
但却互相听不到声音，
我愿跟随着月光
到千里之外去照拂着你。
大雁呀
总是在飞
可是，月光传不来他的音信，
鱼龙潜跃在江底
空皱出一层层波纹。
昨夜
我梦见在安静的潭水里
飘着片片落花，
可怜
春天过了大半
也没见他回家。

江水呀
流送着春天，春天将尽，
可是
江潭里的落月
还是要西斜。
西斜的月亮
沉落隐藏在那一片茫茫海雾中，
碣石呵
潇湘呵
是望不尽的山远水长的路。
呵
不知道
乘着明月
有几人已归？
落月摇荡着
那愁人的离情和满江的树！

She sees the moon,but her husband is out of sight;

She would follow the moonbeams to shine on his face.

But message-bearing swans can't fly out of moonlight,

Nor letter-sending fish can leap out of their place.

He dreamed of flowers falling o'er the pool last night.

Alas! Spring has half gone,he cannot homeward go.

The water bearing spring will run away in flight;

The moon over the pool in the west will sink low.

In the mist on the sea the slanting moon will hide;

It's a long way from northern hill to southern streams.

How many can go home by moonlight on the tide?

O'er riverside trees the setting moon sheds but dreams.

行 路 难

李 白

其 一

金樽清酒斗十千，玉盘珍羞直万钱。
停杯投箸不能食，拔剑四顾心茫然。
欲渡黄河冰塞川，将登太行雪满山。
闲来垂钓碧溪上，忽复乘舟梦日边。
行路难！行路难！多歧路，今安在？
长风破浪会有时，直挂云帆济沧海。

今译

金酒杯中清洌的美酒
一斗就价值十千，
玉盘里珍贵的佳肴
更是价高万钱。
放下酒杯，停下筷子
吃喝不下，
拔出宝剑，放眼四望
心里一片茫然。
本想渡过黄河
无奈坚冰堵塞了河川，
将要登上太行山巅
可茫茫大雪呀，落满了山。
闲下心来

我要效仿吕尚在溪边垂钓，
又忽然梦见乘着船
像伊尹一样，走过日月之边。
行路难哪，行路难！
那么多的岔路
我要走的路在哪面？
我坚信
乘长风破万里浪的日子
一定会来到，
那时，我要挂起高插入云的
风帆
去横渡苍茫的大海。

HARD IS THE WAY

Li Bai

I

Pure wine in golden cup costs ten thousand coins—good!
Choice dish in plate of jade is worth as much—nice food!
Pushing aside my cup and chopsticks, I can't eat;
Drawing my sword and looking around, I stamp my feet.
I can't cross Yellow River: ice has stopped its flow;
I can't climb Taihang: the mountain is covered with snow.
I can but poise a fishing pole beside a stream
Or set sail for the sun like a sage in a dream.
Hard is the way,
Hard is the way.
Don't go astray!
Whither today?
A time will come to ride the wind and cleave the waves;
I'll set my cloud-white sail and cross the sea that raves.

茅屋为秋风所破歌

杜 甫

八月秋高风怒号，卷我屋上三重茅。
茅飞渡江洒江郊，高者挂罥长林梢，
下者飘转沉塘坳。南村群童欺我老无力，
忍能对面为盗贼。公然抱茅入竹去，
唇焦口燥呼不得，归来倚杖自叹息。

今 译

八月
天那么高
萧瑟的秋风在门外怒号，
好大的风呵，
它吹呀，吹呀
竟卷走了我屋上的那三重
白茅！
茅草飞将起来
渡过江去
洒落在江郊，
高的挂在林子的树梢头，
低的飘转沉浸在那池塘坳。

南村那群小孩儿
也欺负我老啦，没有了气力，
竟忍心这样
面对着面当起强盗！
他们明目张胆抱走我屋上的
茅草
跑到那竹丛里去，
我呼喊得口干舌燥
他们也不答理，
没有办法
回得家来
只好挂着藜杖独自叹息！

MY COTTAGE UNROOFED BY AUTUMN GALE

Du Fu

In the eighth moon the autumn gales furiously howl,

They roll up three layers of straw from my thatched bower.

The straw flies across the river and spreads in shower,

Some hanging knotted on the top of trees which tower,

Some swirling down and sinking into water foul.

Urchins from southern village know I'm old and weak;

They rob me to my face without a blush on cheek;

Holding armfuls of straw,into bamboos they sneak.

In vain I call them till my lips are parched and dry,

Again alone,I lean on my cane and sigh.

俄顷风定云墨色，秋天漠漠向昏黑。
布衾多年冷似铁，娇儿恶卧踏里裂。
床头屋漏无干处，雨脚如麻未断绝。
自经丧乱少睡眠，长夜沾湿何由彻！
安得广厦千万间，大庇天下寒士俱欢颜，
风雨不动安如山。呜呼！
何时眼前突兀见此屋，吾庐独破受冻死亦足！

今译

转眼间
风停了下来
云层忽然变成了墨色，
那沉暗迷濛的天空
也眼看就要昏黑。
呵
粗布的棉被
盖了多年
冷得就像块铁，
孩子们横躺竖卧
把被里子也给蹬破蹯裂。
屋子漏
床铺下没一处是干爽的地方，
洒落着的雨脚
密得就像麻似的
而且没有断歇。
我自从变乱以来
就很少睡眠，
在这样漫长的夜晚
湿漉漉、黏糊糊地

让我怎样才能挨到天亮？
呵
从哪儿才能够
得到一座宽大的屋子
有千间万间？
好保护着天下所有寒苦的读书人
叫他们
个个都能有个欢笑的脸；
不论是风吹
还是雨打
他们都能安稳得像泰山一般！
唉，唉
什么时候
在眼前
真能耸现出这样一座大屋，
等到那时候
就是独有我这茅屋房子被吹破
让我受冻乃至冻死
我也将心满意足！

Shortly the gale subsides and clouds turn dark as ink;

The autumn skies are shrouded and in darkness sink.

My cotton quilt is cold:for years it has been worn;

My restless children kick in sleep and it is torn.

The roof leaks o'er beds,leaving no corner dry,

Without cease the rain falls thick and fast from the sky.

After the troubled times troubled has been my sleep.

Wet through,how can I pass the night so long,so deep!

Could I get mansions covering ten thousand miles,

I'd house all scholars poor and make them beam with smiles.

In wind and rain these mansions would stand like mountains high.

Alas!Should these houses appear before my eye,

Frozen in my unroofed cot,content I'd die.

白雪歌送武判官归京

岑 参

北风卷地白草折，胡天八月即飞雪。
忽如一夜春风来，千树万树梨花开。
散入珠帘湿罗幕，狐裘不暖锦衾薄。
将军角弓不得控，都护铁衣冷难著。

今译

北风呜呜地，卷地而来
塞外的白草呵，已经被吹折，
这北方的八月
便开始下起大雪。
呵
那大雪
飘落在枝枝桠桠上
就像一夜之间春风吹来，
千千万万棵梨树上
忽然之间，那梨花全都绽开。
呵，大雪呀
飞进垂挂的珠帘，打湿了罗幕，
穿着狐狸皮裘
也不觉得温暖
盖着锦衾，都感到单薄。
将军的双手被冻得
连角弓都无法拉开，
天寒地冻，冷呵
连主帅的那铁衣
都难再穿着。

SONG OF WHITE SNOW IN FAREWELL TO SECRETARY WU GOING BACK TO THE CAPITAL

Cen Shen

Snapping the pallid grass,the northern wind whirls low;

In the eighth moon the Tartar sky is filled with snow.

As if the vernal breeze had come back overnight,

Adorning thousands of pear trees with blossoms white.

Flakes enter pearled blinds and wet the silken screen;

Nor furs of fox can warm us nor brocade quilts green.

The general cannot draw his rigid bow with ease,

And the commissioner in coat of mail would freeze.

瀚海阑干百丈冰，愁云惨淡万里凝。
中军置酒饮归客，胡琴琵琶与羌笛。
纷纷暮雪下辕门，风掣红旗冻不翻。
轮台东门送君去，去时雪满天山路。
山回路转不见君，雪上空留马行处。

今译

在海一样无边无际的大沙漠上
纵横交错着
高达百丈的冰柱，
令人发愁的寒云
惨惨淡淡
举目万里，就仿佛被冻凝。
在中军帐里
摆起酒宴
为了欢送你这位归客，
有助饮的胡琴和琵琶
还有羌笛。
傍晚
那一天大雪呀
纷纷扬扬，飘落在辕门，

风呵
撕掣着红色的军旗
那军旗也结了冰，再不能翻动。
呵
在轮台城的东门
我送你——
送你东去，
你离去的时候
那一天大雪呀
都封了天山古路。
山回路转
已经再看不见了你的踪影
这时候
那片雪地上
只留下你们那一行人
走过的马蹄足迹！

A thousand feet o'er cracked wilderness ice piles,

And gloomy clouds hang sad and drear for miles and miles.

We drink in headquarters to our guest homeward bound;

With Tartar flutes, pipas and pipes the camps resound.

At dusk snow in large flakes falls heavy on camp gate;

The frozen red flag in the wind won't undulate.

At eastern gate of Wheel Tower we bid goodbye

When snow covers the road to Heaven's Mountain high.

I watch his horse go past a bend and, lost to sight,

His track will soon be buried by snow in flight.

琵琶行

白居易

浔阳江头夜送客，枫叶荻花秋瑟瑟。
主人下马客在船，举酒欲饮无管弦。
醉不成欢惨将别，别时茫茫江浸月。
忽闻水上琵琶声，主人忘归客不发。
寻声暗问弹者谁，琵琶声停欲语迟。
移船相近邀相见，添酒回灯重开宴。
千呼万唤始出来，犹抱琵琶半遮面。

今译

夜晚
在浔阳江头
我送行客，
枫叶呵
荻花呀
在秋风里萧萧索索。
主人下马
走进行客的船
举起杯
想饮酒
却没有管弦。
醉了
也没有一点欢乐
而又将凄凄惨惨地分别，
分别时
眼前迷迷茫茫
大江在浸润着一轮明月。
忽然听到
从水上传来琵琶之声，

主人忘了归去
客船也不想出发。
寻着声
悄悄探问
弹琵琶的是谁，
琵琶声停了
虽想回答，又迟迟疑疑
划动船
挨过去
邀弹者出来相见，
添酒加菜
点起灯来
又重新开宴。
千遍呼
万遍唤
她才慢慢出来，
还抱着琵琶
一半遮着脸。

SONG OF A *PIPA* PLAYER

Bai Juyi

One night by riverside I bade a friend goodbye;
In maple leaves and rushes autumn seemed to sigh.
My friend and I dismounted and came into the boat;
We wished to drink but there was no music afloat.
Without flute songs we drank our cups with heavy heart;
The moonbeams blent with water when we were to part.
Suddenly o'er the stream we heard a *pipa* lute sound;
I forgot to go home and the guest stood spell-bound.
We followed where the music led to find the player,
But heard the *pipa* stop and no music in the air.
We moved our boat near the musician's to invite
The player to the replenished feast by lamplight.
Again and again we urged her to appear until
She came, her face half hid behind a *pipa* still.

转轴拨弦三两声,未成曲调先有情。
弦弦掩抑声声思,似诉平生不得意。
低眉信手续续弹,说尽心中无限事。
轻拢慢捻抹复挑,初为霓裳后绿腰。
大弦嘈嘈如急雨,小弦切切如私语。
嘈嘈切切错杂弹,大珠小珠落玉盘。
间关莺语花底滑,幽咽泉流冰下难。
冰泉冷涩弦凝绝,凝绝不通声暂歇。

今译

转动着轴
拨弄着弦
弹响了三声两声,
还未构成曲调
已露出感情。
弦弦掩抑
声声都充满情思,
就好像在倾诉着
她平生是如何的不得志。
低着眉
信着手
继续弹,
诉尽心中无限的
伤心往事。
轻轻地拢
慢慢地捻
抹而又挑,
最初弹的是《霓裳羽衣舞曲》
后来弹的是《绿腰》。
大弦呵
十分急促

嘈嘈切切,就像骤雨,
小弦呵
十分舒缓,就如在悄悄私语。
忽而急促
忽而舒缓
高低快慢杂着弹,
就像大小珍珠
叮叮当当
落进玉盘。
一会儿唧唧喳喳
如莺声燕语
在花间流转,
一会儿幽幽咽咽
就像流泉
迟缓地流在河滩。
泉水哪
又冷又涩
好像那弦都要凝绝,
凝绝
像水流不通
声音忽然渐渐停歇。

She turned the pegs and tested twice or thrice each string;
Before a tune was played we heard her feelings sing.
Then note on note she struck with pathos deep and strong;
It seemed to say she'd missed her dreams all her life long.
Head bent, she played with unpremeditated art,
On and on to pour out her overflowing heart.
She lightly plucked, slowly stroked and twanged loud
The song of "Green Waist" after that of "Rainbow Cloud".
The thick strings loudly thrummed like the pattering rain;
The fine strings softly tinkled in murmuring strain.
When mingling loud and soft notes were together played,
'T was like large and small pearls dropping on plate of jade,
Now clear like orioles warbling under flowers nice,
Then sobbing like a stream running beneath the ice.
The stream seemed so icy as to tighten the string;
From tightened strings on more sound could be heard to ring.

别有幽愁暗恨生，此时无声胜有声。
银瓶乍破水浆迸，铁骑突出刀枪鸣。
曲终收拨当心画，四弦一声如裂帛。
东船西舫悄无言，惟见江心秋月白。
沉吟放拨插弦中，整顿衣裳起敛容。
自言本是京城女，家在虾蟆陵下住。
十三学得琵琶成，名属教坊第一部。
曲罢曾教善才伏，妆成每被秋娘妒。
五陵年少争缠头，一曲红绡不知数。
钿头云篦击节碎，血色罗裙翻酒污。

今译

别有一种幽怨
暗暗地，百恨俱生，
这时候
没有声
反而胜过了有声。
忽然
就像银瓶
乍破了
水浆在四处迸溅，
又像千军万马
突入敌阵
刀枪剑戟齐鸣。
曲子弹完了
她用弦拨在胸前
猛然一划
四根弦子
同时发出声来
就如裂帛。
这时候
东船西舫
都悄然无声，
惟一能望见的
只有江中的秋月通明。
她一边叹息

一边放下拨子插进弦中，
整一整衣裳
站了起来
收敛起面容。
自己说：
"奴家本是京城之女，
在虾蟆陵下居住。
十三岁
学琵琶，学得有成，
名字排在教坊的第一部。
演奏的曲子
常常叫那些高手佩服，
由于貌美
梳洗打扮起来
常常会被同班姐妹们嫉妒。
五陵的王孙公子们
都争着赏赐财和物，
一曲弹罢
收到的红绡都难计其数。
按拍子击节
常常把金花银篦敲碎，
饮酒作乐
也常常把血红色罗裙染污。

Still we heard hidden grief and vague regret concealed;
Music expressed then far less than silence revealed.
Suddenly we heard water burst a silver jar,
The clash of spears and sabres coming from afar.
She made a central sweep when the music was ending;
The four strings made one sound, as of silk one is rending.
Silence reigned left and right of the boat, east and west;
We saw but autumn moon white in the river's breast.
She slid the plectrum pensively between the strings,
Smoothed out her dress and rose with a composed mien.
"I spent," she said, "in capital my early springs,
Where at the foot of Mount of Toads my home had been.
At thirteen I learned on the *pipa* how to play,
And my name was among the primas of the day.
I won my master's admiration for my skill;
My beauty was envied by women of ill will.
Gallant young men vied to shower gifts on me;
And one tune played, to give me silk rolls they were free.
Beating time, I let silver comb and pin drop down,
And spilt-out wine oft stained my blood-red silken gown.

今年欢笑复明年，秋月春风等闲度。
弟走从军阿姨死，暮去朝来颜色故。
门前冷落车马稀，老大嫁作商人妇。
商人重利轻别离，前月浮梁买茶去。
去来江口守空船，绕船月明江水寒。
夜深忽梦少年事，梦啼妆泪红阑干！
我闻琵琶已叹息，又闻此语重唧唧。
同是天涯沦落人，相逢何必曾相识！
我从去年辞帝京，谪居卧病浔阳城。
浔阳地僻无音乐，终岁不闻丝竹声。

今译

今年欢笑
明年依旧是欢笑，
秋月呵
春风呵
一年一年过去
都等于虚度。
弟弟从军走了
阿姨又病故，
暮去朝来
我的容颜一天天衰老。
这时候
门前冷落了
车马也稀少了，
年龄大了
只好嫁给一个商人。
商人只注重金钱
不注重别离，
上个月
到浮梁贩运茶叶去了。
只留下我一个人守着空船
明月绕着船舱呵
江水映着月亮
夜晚很冷很冷。

夜深了
睡不好觉
忽然想起青春年少时那些欢乐的事，
梦里，涕泪纵横
都会染污我的容颜。"
我听到琵琶
已经引起叹息，
又听到这一番倾诉
更加感到悲戚。
唉
想我们
同都是这天涯沉沦落魄之人，
如今相逢就相逢了
又何必一定要曾经相识。
我自从去年
离开了长安——那帝京，
被贬后
就卧病在这座浔阳古城。
浔阳古城呵
地处荒僻，没有什么音乐，
整年的
都听不到一点管弦之声。

From year to year I laughed my joyful life away
On moonlit autumn night as windy vernal day.
My younger brother left for war,and died my maid;
Days passed,nights came,and my beauty began to fade.
Fewer and fewer were cabs and steeds at my door;
I married a smug merchant when my prime was o'er.
The merchant cared for money much more than for me;
One month ago he went away to purchase tea.
Leaving his lonely wife alone in empty boat;
Shrouded in moonlight,on the cold river I float.
Deep in the night I dreamed of happy bygone years
And woke to find my rouged face crisscrossed with tears."
Listening to her music,I sighed with pain;
Hearing her story,I sighed again and again.
"Both of us in misfortune go from shore to shore,"
"Meeting now,need we have known each other before?
I was banished from the capital last year
To live degraded and ill in this city here.
The city's too remote to know melodious song,

住近湓江地低湿，黄芦苦竹绕宅生。
其间旦暮闻何物，杜鹃啼血猿哀鸣。
春江花朝秋月夜，往往取酒还独倾。
岂无山歌与村笛？呕哑嘲哳难为听。
今夜闻君琵琶语，如听仙乐耳暂明。
莫辞更坐弹一曲，为君翻作琵琶行。
感我此言良久立，却坐促弦弦转急。
凄凄不似向前声，满座重闻皆掩泣。
座中泣下谁最多，江州司马青衫湿。

今译

住近地势低洼，十分潮湿的湓江口，
黄芦呵
苦竹呵
围绕着住宅丛生。
这里呀
从早到晚能听到什么，
惟有那——
杜鹃啼血，和猿猴的哀鸣。
无论是在花开的清晨
还是在秋江的月明之夜，
往往取酒
自斟自饮。
哪里是没有山歌和村笛，
只是那声音杂乱破碎
实在难听。
只有今夜
听到了你弹的琵琶曲，
有如听见了仙乐
这耳朵突然感到又清又明。
不要推辞

再坐下来，弹上一曲，
好让我
按照那曲调
为你写下一首《琵琶行》。
听到我这话
她很感动
有好长一阵子在旁站立，
随后回到座位
拧紧琵琶弦
弹的弦声愈加急。
这时候
凄凄楚楚的
已不像先前的那弦声，
满座的人
重新听着
都忍不住掩面哭泣。
在座的人中
谁的眼泪流得最多？
是我这个江州司马呀
青衫都被泪水浸湿！

So I have never heard music the whole year long.
I dwell by riverbank on a low and damp ground
In a house yellow reeds and stunt'd bamboos surround.
What is here to be heard from daybreak till nightfall
But gibbon's cry and cuckoo's homeward-going call?
By blooming riverside and under autumn moon
I've often taken wine up and drunk it alone.
Though I have mountain songs and village pipes to hear,
Yet they are crude and strident and grate on the ear.
Listening to you playing on *pipa* tonight,
With music divine even my hearing seems bright.
Will you sit down and play for us a tune once more?
I'll write for you an ode to the *pipa* I adore."
Touched by what I said, the player stood for long,
Then sat down, tore at strings and played another song.
So sad, so drear, so different, it moved us deep;
Those who heard it hid the face and began to weep.
Of all the company at table who wept most?
It was none other than the exiled blue-robed host.

渔 翁

柳宗元

渔翁夜傍西岩宿,
晓汲清湘燃楚竹。
烟销日出不见人,
欸乃一声山水绿。
回看天际下中流,
岩上无心云相逐。

今译

那个老渔翁
傍晚把船靠在西山过宿,
天亮了,打上清洌的湘江水,
又点燃那楚地的湘妃竹。
炊烟消失,旭日东升
却不见他的人影,
"欸乃"一声,一曲棹歌
从青山绿水中传出。
回头远看,水天相接处
只见那小舟顺流而下,
这时候
山岩上的朵朵白云
缭绕舒展,正在相互追逐。

A FISHERMAN

Liu Zongyuan

Under west cliff a fisherman passes the night;

At dawn he makes bamboo fire to boil water clean.

Mist clears off at sunrise but there's no man in sight;

Only the fisherman's song turns hill and rill green.

He goes down mid-stream and turns to look on the sky.

What does he see but clouds freely wafting on high.

图书在版编目(CIP)数据

新编千家诗/袁行霈编;徐放,韩珊今译;许渊冲英译.
北京:中华书局,2007
(大中华文库)
ISBN 7-101-04940-0

Ⅰ.新… Ⅱ.①袁…②徐…③韩…④许… Ⅲ.①英语—汉语—对照读物②古典诗歌—作品集—中国 Ⅳ.H319.4:Ⅰ

中国版本图书馆 CIP 数据核字(2005)第 137633 号

责任编辑:齐浣心

大中华文库
新编千家诗
许渊冲　英译
徐放　韩珊　今译

©2007　中华书局
出版发行者:
中华书局
　　(北京市丰台区太平桥西里 38 号　100073)
　　http://www.zhbc.com.cn
　　E-mail:zhbc@zhbc.com.cn
印制者:
深圳佳信达印务有限公司印刷
开本:960×640　1/16(精装)　印张:21.75　印数:5500 册
2007 年 12 月第 1 版第 2 次印刷
(汉英) ISBN 7-101-04940-0/I·672
定价:54.00 元

版权所有　盗版必究